ANNO DOMINI

JESUS THROUGH THE CENTURIES

∾ *Exploring the Heart of Two Millennia* ∾

DAVID J. GOA, LINDA DISTAD, AND MATTHEW WANGLER

THE PROVINCIAL MUSEUM OF ALBERTA

ANNO DOMINI

JESUS THROUGH THE CENTURIES

❧ Exploring the Heart of Two Millennia ❧

DAVID J. GOA, LINDA DISTAD,
AND MATTHEW WANGLER

AND CONTRIBUTIONS BY
BENJAMIN L. BERGER, DELLA DENNIS, FRIEDA WOODRUFF GRAMIT,
KAREN MULDER, AND ANGELA TARANGER

A publication of
The Provincial Museum of Alberta
Edmonton, Alberta, Canada, 2000

*Anno Domini: Jesus Through
the Centuries* is produced by the
Provincial Museum of Alberta
and is held at the museum,
7 October 2000 – 7 January 2001.
The curator of the exhibition is
David J. Goa. Jaroslav Pelikan,
Sterling Professor Emeritus,
Yale University is the Honorary
Curator of this exhibition.

Alberta Community Development
Millennium Bureau of Canada
Canadian Heritage Information
 Network, Canadian Heritage
Museums Assistance Programme,
 Canadian Heritage
Canadian Broadcasting Corporation
Edmonton Community Foundation

Central image on cover:
CHRIST PANTOCRATOR, 1994.
Heiko Schlieper, 1931-.
Secco in St George the Victory
Bearer Ukrainian Catholic Church,
Edmonton. Photograph by
David J. Goa.

Central image on title-page:
SCENES FROM THE
LIFE OF JESUS, CIRCA 1850.
Silver pectoral cross.
Russian Orthodox. The Provincial
Museum of Alberta [H85.1206.3].

Goa, David J.
Anno Domini : Jesus through the centuries. Gallery guide

Catalogue of an exhibition held at the Provincial Museum of Alberta.
ISBN 0-7785-1232-0

1. Jesus Christ—Art—Exhibitions. I. Distad, Linda. II. Wangler,
Matthew. III. Provincial Museum of Alberta. IV. Title.
N8050.G62 2000 Suppl.   704.9'4853'074712334   C00-910752-5

TABLE OF CONTENTS

ALTHOUGH I CANNOT SAY WITH CERTAINTY, IT SEEMS PLAUSIBLE TO ME THAT THE NAME OF JESUS WAS ONE OF THE FIRST NAMES I SPOKE AS A CHILD, AND THIS NO DOUBT WAS THE OCCASION OF MODEST REJOICING BY MY MOTHER AND FATHER.

At table or in my father's carpentry-shop, while walking on the pathways of our modest provincial city or planting the garden on Victoria Day, in church or pondering the tragedies, struggles, and joys of neighbours, friends, and strangers, considering the martyrdom of Gandhi or the Cold War and a myriad of other events equally compelling, the name of him who "holds all things together" was never far from the lips of my parents and their friends. As a child I knew Jesus welcomed the friendship of children along the pathways of Galilee and in Jerusalem, that he said the kingdom of God was in some strange way present in my being and that of my playmates, and that he compelled his followers to learn from the delight of children in the wonder of the world and welcome their curiosity and their struggles. As a father and adult I have daily glimpsed the beauty, truth, and goodness of this simple insight. Jesus' stories and parables, his compassion and openness to others – strangers as well as friends and disciples – fascinated my young mind and called me to ponder both my own adult life and that of the world in which I lived and worked. His critique of authority, "of business as usual" in his society and culture, has pricked my conscience and provided an alternative to "how we should then live." The more I have come to know of the shaping and reshaping of culture and civilization, of "the image of Jesus created by each successive epoch," the more I have come to see him as a "key to understanding the temper and values of each of these epochs" as Jaroslav Pelikan has put it. In my view, this is one way of understanding, with a little more breadth and depth, how we have come to be the way we are at the beginning of the third millennium. This way is central and of enormous significance, but it is by no means the only way.

I first met Jaroslav Pelikan as a boy of eleven when my father gave me what I thought was his first book, *Fools for Christ: Essays on the True, the Good, and the Beautiful* (1955) to read. It was followed quickly by what I later learned was his first book, *From Luther to Kierkegaard: A Study in the History of Theology* (1950). His monumental study, *The Christian Tradition: A History of the Development of Doctrine* (1971-1989), has been a constant companion since the University of Chicago Press published each of the five volumes. I read *Jesus Through the Centuries: His Place in the History of Culture* shortly after Yale University Press published it in 1985, but it was not until 1986 that I was privileged to meet Professor Pelikan. As a result of my own field research work on Eastern Christian liturgical life and a growing sense of the dearth of scholarship on the living tradition of Eastern Christianity in North America, I brought together a group of scholars to address a portion of this theme on the millennium of the Christianization of Kievan Rus'. This was made possible through the good offices of the Canadian Institute of Ukrainian Studies at the University of Alberta. I invited Professor Pelikan to come to Edmonton in March, 1986, to speak on "Eastern Christianity in Modern Culture: Genius and Dilemma" as a keynote for our reflections. This paper, along with others, I was pleased to edit into the volume *The Ukrainian Religious Experience: Tradition and the Canadian Cultural Context* (1989), the fruit of our work over those three days in March. For the same commemoration I did an exhibition, *Seasons of Celebration: Ritual in Eastern Christian Culture*, at The Provincial Museum of Alberta and published a catalogue under the same title for which Professor Pelikan wrote a foreword. That exhibition toured every province in Canada except Prince Edward Island from 1986-1989.

Following a brief correspondence on the idea of an exhibition on the theme of "Jesus Through the Centuries" Professor Pelikan and I met in 1994 at the Yale Club, across from Grand Central Station in New York, for a day's conversation on the idea. I was a little surprised that no large and prestigious museum or art gallery had proposed such an exhibition to Professor Pelikan. The reasons are perhaps obvious. Museums and art galleries in North America have focused on connoisseur exhibitions, showing fine works of art or examining an artist's work or particular school of art in retrospect. Museums devoted to the study of history and culture have been very shy when it comes to the religious dimensions of North American culture, unless they have to do with a community or tradition that the popular culture deems exotic. Rarely have museums given the public an occasion to glimpse the large themes that have shaped and reshaped Western civilization. The cultural climate, and particularly that of academe, in the last thirty years has been occupied with the critique of the roots of European culture and particularly its tap-root in Jerusalem. It has become difficult to speak about the contribution and role the cardinal ideas, images, stories, and texts have in shaping the gifts of the West. The reasons for this climate are not difficult to understand and the impulse for much of it is laudable. But I have noticed, as have many other scholars and cultural critics, that this period, which some have characterized as the "decline of the West," has left us, as we enter the third millennium, with a generation or two completely unfamiliar with those ideas, images, stories, and texts that spring from the ways Jesus has been understood over twenty centuries.

An exhibition of this kind requires, first, a deep regard for questions of the continuity of its theme, questions that are at the heart of our honorary curator Professor Pelikan's work. The Christian tradition has long proclaimed that "Jesus is the same yesterday, today and forever" and, while that idea has been used all too often to justify cultural vandalism, it is also at the heart of many of the gifts of Christian culture and civilization, gifts now shared throughout much of the world. The second requirement is a regard for the enormous pluralism flowering from the influence of Jesus over two millennia and the embodiments of this influence from Norway to South Africa, from Brazil to India. While it is clearly impossible to do such a matter full justice in even a large suite of exhibitions, it also seemed to me that the year 2000 offers us an opportunity to glimpse the significance of this theme in a modest way. *Anno Domini: Jesus Through the Centuries* is our way of marking the beginning of the third millennium by reflecting on the footprints of Jesus who walked the pathways of Galilee 2,000 ago.

Anno Domini: Jesus Through the Centuries invites us to glimpse some of the ways Jesus has been understood and how this understanding has shaped and reshaped culture. I have also been concerned that he "who is ever ancient, ever new" not be confined to the past or colonized by any particular period or perspective. Each of the images of Jesus, whether Rabbi, King of Kings, or Liberator, that came to the forefront of a particular epoch in Western history has remained part of the cache of ideas that continues to form and inform Western civilization and world cultures down to the present age. For this reason modern artistic works appear in most of the theme areas. Whatever else one may make of the Christian tradition, it remains a living tradition. Jesus' teaching has echoed in the works and deeds of many poets and novelists, as well as church and secular leaders and political activists throughout the twentieth century. "Voices of the Twentieth Century," a suite of banners throughout the exhibition, allow the words of men and women who, knowingly or not, joined their voices to that of Jesus.

Anno Domini is a cultural exhibition, not an art exhibition. Also, it explores not what Jesus *meant*, for that is the province of Christians and Churches, but what his person and teaching *has been taken to mean*. Since Alberta has become home to Christians from all parts of Europe, Asia, Africa, and Latin America over the last century, and since its cultural landscape reflects the pluralism of this grand tradition, it is perhaps appropriate that this exhibition is born of the soil of our province. As Curator of Folklife I have built the sources of knowledge about our many cultural communities within the collections of The Provincial Museum of Alberta. The field research studies have focused on memory, living tradition, historical experience, and sense of place. These encounters over a quarter century have provided local ground to nourish this project. My work in Jewish, Muslim, Hindu, Buddhist, and Sikh communities during this period has heightened my regard for the worlds of meaning each generation draws on as it faces its own day. It is my friends and colleagues within these communities, and their encouragement, interest, and knowledge of just how significant the Christian tradition has been to the shaping of our nation, that has helped me address the many questions about the value of this exhibition and given me the courage to continue.

As the reader may note, many have contributed to this exhibition. Linda Distad has joined in the research, writing, and editorial work and made what was a daunting task possible. She cannot be thanked enough for her enormous contribution under often demanding circumstances. My young colleagues Andru McCracken and Matthew Wangler have been singularly committed to our work and brought their consummate skills to bear on each new issue. Paul Beier, the designer of the exhibition, has worked his particular magic. They, along with W. Bruce McGillivray, who has smoothed the many administrative pathways, have brought *Anno Domini: Jesus Through the Centuries* to fruition.

A final note of gratitude goes to those who have taught me the significance of the encounter with Jesus over twenty centuries, and particularly to Jaroslav Pelikan for his elegant synthesis and gracious spirit. ❧

David J. Goa, Curator of Folklife

When Jesus saw the crowds, he went up the mountain; and after he sat down, his disciples came to him. Then he began to speak, and taught them, saying: "Blessed are the poor in spirit, for theirs is the kingdom of heaven. "Blessed are those who mourn, for they will be comforted. "Blessed are the meek, for they will inherit the earth. "Blessed are those who hunger and thirst for righteousness, for they will be filled. "Blessed are the merciful, for they will receive mercy. "Blessed are the pure in heart, for they will see God. "Blessed are the peacemakers, for they will be called children of God. "Blessed are you when people revile you and persecute you and utter all kinds of evil against you falsely on my account. Rejoice and be glad, for your reward is great in heaven, for in the same way they persecuted the prophets who were before you."

Matthew 5:1-12

The introductory video for *Anno Domini* explores how the life and teachings of Jesus are incarnated in the events of the world that flash upon our television screens. The video is structured around the ideas of the Beatitudes, a portion of Jesus' Sermon on the Mount. The Beatitudes provide an elegant and poignant reflection upon the realities of the human condition – the tragedies of living in a "vale of tears," and the graceful efforts of those who have sought to bring peace and joy to a broken world. Regardless of whether one follows him, Jesus has the powerful ability to speak to the people of the world about the realities of their lives.

BLESSED ARE THE MEEK...

GANDHI (1869-1948)
Mohandas Gandhi employed the most radical of weapons – non-violence – in his efforts to liberate India from British colonial rule.

JEAN VANIER (1928-)
Jean Vanier is a philosopher, theologian, and the founder of L'Arche, an international organization that creates community among the mentally and physically disabled and those who work with them.

BLESSED ARE THOSE WHO MOURN...

SCHOOL SHOOTING IN TABER, ALBERTA (1999)
In a morbid re-enactment of the Columbine shootings, a 14-year-old boy opened fire at W. R. Myers High School in Taber, Alberta, wounding one student and killing another, Jason Lang, son of local Anglican minister, Reverend Dale Lang.

MONTREAL MASSACRE
On 6 December 1989, a lone gunman, Marc Lepine, walked into the École Polytechnique in Montreal and opened fire. Lepine murdered fourteen women before taking his own life.

NORTHERN IRELAND
Northern Ireland has long been split along cultural, political, and religious lines. The current cycle of violence between the two sides began in 1968. A tenuous peace currently exists in the area.

Blessed are the pure in heart...

Aimee Semple McPherson (1890-1944)
Canadian-born evangelist Aimee Semple McPherson was the founder of the International Church of the Foursquare Gospel and was renowned for her passionate, flashy sermons.

Mother Teresa (1910-1997)
Initially a school teacher in Calcutta, Mother Teresa was moved by the abject poverty and destitution of those outside the walls of her classroom to found her own religious order, the Missionaries of Charity, to care for the sick and suffering.

Blessed are the merciful...

Robert Latimer
In 1997, Saskatchewan farmer Robert Latimer was convicted of the 1994 killing of his 12-year-old daughter, Tracy. Tracy had suffered from a severe form of cerebral palsy and Latimer said he ended her life to release her from her constant agony.

Karla Faye Tucker (1959-1998)
On 3 February 1998 Karla Faye Tucker was executed in Texas for her part in two savage murders committed in 1983. Formerly a heavy drug user and prostitute, Tucker became a born-again Christian while imprisoned.

Blessed are those who hunger and thirst for righteousness...

Nelson Mandela (1918-)
Nelson Mandela has spent decades – many of them in prison – fighting for the establishment of a non-racial society in South Africa founded upon democracy, equality, and education. In 1994, Mandela became the first democratically elected State President of South Africa.

Tommy Douglas (1904-1986)
Tommy Douglas fought passionately for the rights of the common people in Canada. Integral in the creation of many key Canadian policies, Douglas is best known for his role in establishing universal medicare in Canada.

Martin Luther King, Jr (1929-1968)
A central figure in the civil rights movement of the 1960s and an American national hero, Martin Luther King, Jr employed the weapons of nonviolent social protest to illuminate the plight of African-Americans and galvanize resistance to racial discrimination.

Blessed are the peacemakers...

The Berlin Wall (1961-1989)
Built in the early 1960s, the Berlin Wall was constructed in order to prevent the inhabitants of Soviet East Berlin from immigrating to democratic West Berlin. In 1989, as a result of changes in Russian foreign policy and domestic pressure in Germany, the Berlin Wall was torn down.

Peace in the Middle East
For decades, the Lebanese, Palestinian, and Jewish communities have struggled around issues of territories and rights. These struggles, motivated in large part by ethnic and religious differences, have often led to simmering tensions and bloodshed in the region. Recently, valiant efforts have been made to establish peace in the region.

African-American Civil Rights Movement
In the 1950s and 1960s, African-Americans agitated for the desegregation of American schools and other institutions. Often violently opposed and jailed, the heroes of the Black civil rights movement continued to pressure government and society for equality and freedom.

Blessed are the persecuted...

Oscar Romero (1917-1980)
Transformed from a bookish conservative into a passionate fighter for justice in El Salvador by the murder of a priest, Oscar Romero was an outspoken critic of the repression of his nation's citizens by the government and military. He was martyred in 1980.

Stephen Biko (1946-1977)
Stephen Biko wanted to liberate the Blacks of South Africa from both the external persecution by the state and the internalization of the ideology of Black inferiority. In 1977, while imprisoned, Biko was murdered by members of the police.

Holocaust Victims
The Holocaust is one of the most horrifying events in the history of the human family. Inflamed by racist propaganda and political rhetoric, the Nazi party and its collaborators coordinated the systematic persecution and extermination of millions of people deemed to be inferior or impure. Six million Jews were murdered during the Holocaust.

Created by David J. Goa and Jeremy Chugg with Matthew Wangler and Andru McCracken.
Produced by Jeremy Chugg of Jeremy Daniel Productions.
Written by David J. Goa.
This video was made possible through a partnership with the Canadian Broadcasting Corporation.

A RUMBLING:

truth itself has appeared among humankind in the very thick of their flurrying metaphors.

Paul Celan

Two millennia of Christian ascendancy have etched Jesus Christ onto the world's symbolic lining. By making him cosmic, divine, and messiah, has he been robbed of his own world? Here is a truth that history has turned into a paradox – Christianity was born of the words of Jesus, Rabbi Jeshua bar-Joseph.

For 2,000 years, Jesus Christ has been the life-blood of the Christian faith. For two millennia, he has lived in the hearts and minds of Christians as the Son of Man, the Incarnation of the Divine, Saviour of the World, indeed, the very meaning of existence. His life and teachings have inspired the largest religious movement the world has ever known. Yet one must wonder if the magnificent grandeur and profound historical significance of Christian culture has perhaps overshadowed the simple fact that Jesus was a Jew. Indeed, a sensitive appreciation of his Jewish formation and context enriches our understanding of much of Jesus' life and teaching. He lived as a Jew, engaging in the spiritual life of the synagogue; he taught as a Jew, his words and methods deeply rooted in Hebrew biblical and rabbinical tradition; and, above all, he was perceived by his followers as the fulfillment of Jewish prophecy. Those who claimed Jesus understood his life as the convergence of a number of archetypal figures of the Hebrew Bible: the King, establishing and maintaining the liberty and dignity of his people; the Sage,

penetrating into the heart of Jewish scripture; the Prophet, urgently invoking Israel to return to God; and the Messiah (or in its Greek form, "Christ"), the Anointed One of God who would redeem his people.

VOICE OF THE TWENTIETH CENTURY

ELIE WIESEL
1928-present

Romania-born survivor of Auschwitz, Buna, Buchenwald, and Gleiwitz. Writer and teacher. Awarded Nobel Peace Prize in 1986. Founder of Elie Wiesel Foundation for Humanity to combat indifference, intolerance, and injustice.

"You think you are suffering for my sake and for my brothers', yet we are the ones who will be made to suffer for you, because of you."

Shlomo, to Jesus on the Cross.

Elie Wiesel, *A Beggar in Jerusalem,* (New York, NY: Avon Books, 1971), 68.

JESUS, THE JEW

JESUS, THE RABBI

Hillel says: "Be among the disciples of Aaron, loving peace and pursuing peace, loving people and bringing them closer to the Torah."

Pirkei Avot, 1:12

The Gospels tell us Jesus offered a fresh approach to interpretation of the Hebrew Bible. So we must see him within a religious culture of intense debate among groups of rabbis. Jesus engaged in these discussions through the rabbinical style of rhetorical question and parable (mashal). Jesus lived in his world as an observant Jew and skilled rabbi but lives in the Christian world's memory as divine.

JESUS, PROPHET AND MESSIAH

Fill the silver goblet;
Make open the door-way;
Let there be no sob; let
Elijah come our way.

And let him come singing,
Announcing as nigh a
Redemption, and drinking
The health of Messiah!

A.M. Klein, "Song"

Some Jews of Jesus' time hoped for transformation of the world by a messiah. Most did not view Jesus as that messiah. Drawing upon the messianic tradition established in the Hebrew Bible, the early Christian community fixed its hopes for redemption on the figure who came to represent the drawing together of the principle motifs of Judaism. In this way Jesus the Rabbi, the prophet, the Jew, became the Christian messiah.

CIRCUMCISION, 1525-1575.
(top) Flemish School. Oil on panel. Netherlands. The Courtauld Gallery, London [CL 125B]. The Jewish ritual of circumcision on the eighth day of an infant's life symbolizes the covenant relationship between God and Israel, and the baby's participation in the continuing unfolding of Creation.

THE PRODIGAL SON, CIRCA 1810.
(far left) Attributed to Friedrich Krebs, 1749-1815. Watercolour on laid paper. Southeastern Pennsylvania. Rare Book Department, The Free Library of Pennsylvania [FLP 30. Borneman]. This parable (mashal) in which Jesus tells the story of a young man who squanders his inheritance, despairs, and is joyfully welcomed home by his father teaches God's love for Israel, the heart of Torah.

TRANSFIGURATION, 1998.
(left) Heiko Schlieper, 1931-. Icon. Canada. Collection Heiko Schlieper. This icon commemorates the Gospel event recorded in each of the synoptic Gospels. The Christian East understands the Transfiguration to speak of a transformed nature (theosis), a glory shared by Moses and Elijah.

"Go out to the whole world; proclaim the Good News to all creation."

Mark 16:16

While Jesus walked the earth, his presence was most deeply felt in his Jewish world. As early Christians carried their message to the Gentile world, and thinkers and artists grappled with the meaning of God's Incarnation, they evolved a "grammar of history." Thus Jesus imparted order and meaning to the flow of time.

What does Jesus mean for our understanding of time, of history, and of the unfolding of our own brief moment in the sweep of time and the eternal? On one level, the answer is obvious. Much of the world dates historical events using a calendar which pivots on the traditional date of Jesus' birth. On a deeper level, we must ask how Jesus understood time and how this understanding has shaped and reshaped our own understanding of time. Readers of the Gospels have often understood Jesus as an apocalyptic prophet calling the men and women of the world to repent of their sins and return to a relationship with the divine before they are overwhelmed and vanquished by the weight of their life-denying actions and thoughts. There has been a tension in the Christian tradition between those who understood the end of history and consequently the meaning of time as a process of linear unfolding of the "plan of God" culminating in the advent of the paradise day, and those who have focused on the presence of the Kingdom of God in this life and the lives of

the saints as the model for living now in communion with God. For Christians amidst these various complex ways of interpreting history and the movement of time, the life of human society and the journey of each person participates in the continuing unveiling of the mystery of the Lord of history.

VOICE OF THE TWENTIETH CENTURY

T. S. ELIOT
1888-1965

Anglo-American poet, critic, and playwright. Active in the Anglo-Catholic movement within the Church of England. Nobel Prize for Literature 1948.

I had seen birth and death, / But had thought they were different; this Birth was / Hard and bitter agony for us, like Death, our death. / We returned to our places, these Kingdoms, / But no longer at ease here, in the old dispensation, / With an alien people clutching their gods. I should be glad at another death.

T. S. Eliot, *"The Journey of the Magi" in The Complete Poems and Plays,* 1909-1950 (New York: Harcourt, Brace & World, 1971), 68-69.

LITTLE DENIS AND THE CHRISTIAN CALENDAR

"The perennial feast days commemorated the Incarnation of our Lord, the occasion of our redemption, and the source of our hope."

Arno Borst,
The Ordering of Time

The first Christians used the Jewish calendar or the Roman system of dating events. Later, they began to date from the "Age of Martyrs" under Emperor Diocletian (284-305). Dionysius Exiguus ("Little Denis," circa 500-550) developed the Christian calendar from a more auspicious date – the birth of Jesus (Anno Domini). He was formally acknowledging the apparent absurdity which the Christian world had long understood – that, symbolically history begins with the birth of a Galilean peasant.

JESUS AND THE LIFE OF THE SAINTS

"…Father, said I, do you see this pitcher lying, a pitcher or whatsoever it may be? And he said, I see it. And I said to him, can it be called by any other name than that which it is? And he answered, no. So can I call myself nought other than that which I am, a Christian."

Vita, Saint Perpetua

Jesus is seen as the turning point of history through his transformative influence on devout Christians. Saint Perpetua converted to Christianity and refused to sacrifice to the Roman gods. While imprisoned, she was strengthened by dreams of her own salvation. In spite of her father's pleas and her anguish at leaving her infant son motherless, Perpetua remained steadfast. In 203, she was executed. Her last worldly act was to kiss a fellow Christian martyr.

APOCALYPSE, ANCIENT AND MODERN

"And the kings of the earth, who committed fornication and were wanton with [the great whore of Babylon], will weep and wail over her when they see smoke of her burning. …And the merchants of the earth weep and mourn for her, since no one buys their cargo any more…."

Revelation 18:9

The delay (or non-occurrence) of the anticipated apocalypse led to a remarkable evolution in Christian consciousness – the coexistence of a hoped for Kingdom of God and the embracing of the unfolding of human history. The fervent anticipation of the Second Coming increasingly accommodated a belief that, through his life, death, and Resurrection, Jesus had already transformed the meaning of human history and existence.

MAP OF THE WORLD WITH JERUSALEM IN THE CENTRE, CIRCA 1275.

(top) Manuscript. England. British Library Manuscript Collections [Add. MS 28681, fol. 9]. From an English psalter, this map showing Jerusalem in the centre of the world reflects the notion that Christ unites heaven and earth, divine and human history.

FASCICULUS TEMPO[RUM] OMNES ANTIQUO[RUM] CRONICAS COMPLECTENS, 1477.

(Below) Werner Rolevinck, 1425-1502. Germany. Collection Nicholas Wickenden. Rolevinck's history of the world is the first to give dates counting backward and forward from the birth of Jesus, expressing Christ's presence throughout all time.

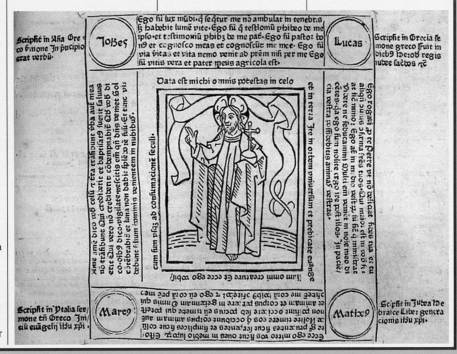

"But what was the sun like, before it came up?"

Walter de la Mare

During the early years the Christian faith turned to interpreting Jesus as the light of revelation long foreshadowed in the cultures of many Gentiles. From the rich cultural cache of Greco-Roman civilization, Christian thinkers seized upon symbols and ideas they believed were arrows directing the Gentile community towards Christ.

As the early followers of Jesus began to carry his message out of the Jewish community and into the Gentile world, they began to see aspects of his message in new places. The intellectual tradition of the Church, from the Acts of the Apostles forward, shows that many of the great ideas and hopes of Gentile communities had been, in a commonly used metaphor, "arrows" pointing to the coming of Christ. Christian thinkers raised on the great Greek and Roman artists, Homer and Virgil, saw in their marvelous works a glimmer of the light which had finally come to them in the fullness of Jesus' Gospel. Is not the image of Odysseus lashed to the mast a foretelling of Jesus nailed to the cross? Doesn't Virgil's description of a coming Golden Age to be ushered in by a child speak in the beautiful language of the ancient Latin peoples of a redemptive birth we now know as the birth of Christ? Indeed, the early Fathers and Mothers of the Church argued, many of the wonderful ideas, images, and stories of Greco-Roman culture have some share in the True, the Good,

and the Beautiful which had finally been revealed in all its radiance in Christ, the Incarnation of God and the fullness of the human nature.

VOICE OF THE TWENTIETH CENTURY

SADHU SUNDAR SINGH
1889-1929

Known as the "Apostle with the Bleeding Feet." Wandered the roads of India in his yellow robe and turban preaching the Gospel of Christ.

I am not worthy to follow in the steps of My Lord, but, like Him, I want no home, No possessions. Sharing the suffering of my People, eating with those who will give me Shelter, and telling all men of the love of God.

John D. Woodbridge, general editor, *Great Leaders of the Christian Church* (Chicago: Moody Press, 1988), 148.

THE GENTILE SAINTS

"And therefore it behooved that blessed Job also, who uttered those high mysteries of His Incarnation, should by his life be a sign of Him ... and by all that he underwent should show forth what were to be His sufferings...."

Gregory the Great,
Moralia on Job

Messianic hope and prophecy were not the exclusive property of the Israelite community. Job, Jethro, and Balaam, who were not Jews, appear within the Hebrew Bible. For the early Church, these "Gentile saints" pointed the way to Christ. Job, the righteous man afflicted with unimaginable suffering testing his faith in God, was of particular importance for Christian theologians and saints. Job was seen as an expression of God's presence in the midst of suffering.

THE MESSIAH ANTICIPATED

Then said the Lady Circe: ..."Square in your ship's path are Sirens, crying beauty to bewitch men coasting by; woe to the innocent who hears that sound! ... the Sirens will sing his mind away on their sweet meadow lolling. ..."

Homer, *Odyssey*
Book XII

Few works of literature provided a more explicit foreshadowing of the life of Jesus than Virgil's *Fourth Eclogue* and Homer's *Odyssey*. Church fathers acknowledged each of them as "prince of poets" and Clement of Alexandria (died circa 215) saw in the image of Odysseus bound to the mast a foreshadowing of Jesus, the *Logos* and Word of God. The cross freed one from the passions and brought one to the safe harbour of paradise.

VIRGIN AND CHILD WITH SAINT CATHERINE(?) AND SAINT JEROME, CA. 1540-65.

(top) Attributed to Polidoro da Lanciano, 1515-1565. Oil on canvas. Italy. The Courtauld Gallery, London [CL 474]. Jerome, ascetic and learned, used his knowledge of Greek, Hebrew, and Latin to translate the Hebrew Bible and New Testament into Latin, known as the Vulgate

JOB ON THE DUNG HEAP, 1998.

(right) Heiko Schlieper, 1931-. Icon. Canada. Collection Hannah Goa. Job's Passion, like that of Jesus, led to the loss of all he valued. His response to the temptation to "curse God and die" was "Though He would slay him, yet shall I love him."

ODYSSEUS LASHED TO THE MAST.

(below) The image of Odysseus lashed to the mast prefigures Christ nailed to the cross in the thought of Clement of Alexandria.

> "Polycarp, Bishop of Smyrna [died circa 155] arrested during a public festival and asked by his accusers: 'What harm is there in saying Caesar is Lord?' He replied, 'For eighty-six years I have been the servant [of Jesus Christ], and he never did me any injury. How then can I blaspheme my King who saved me?' He was burned at the stake."

Martyrium Polycarpi

When Pontius Pilate asked Jesus if he were a king, he asked a question that has absorbed thinkers. If he is a king, what sort of kingdom does he rule? Much debate has raged and much blood has been spilled over the issues which Jesus' kingship poses.

For nearly three centuries after Christ's death, Christians in the Roman Empire were forced to live through periods of persecution. Christians who refused to worship the gods of Rome or the Emperor were subject to brutal punishments. Then, in 313, the Roman Emperor Constantine I, according to legend, having been inspired by a vision of the cross on the eve of battle, ended the persecution of Christians, adopted Christianity as one of the official religions of the Empire, and, eventually, converted. The same empire which had crucified Christ now publicly embraced him as their spiritual leader and, often, as justification for the temporal exercise of Imperial power. For 1,500 years, even after the fall of the Roman Empire in the east, the intimate connection between Christian faith and political power dominated European culture. Kings asserted the "divine right" of their rule, popes wielded tremendous temporal power, and the distinction between religious and political authority was reshaped.

The political influence of Christianity has undoubtedly waned in the last few centuries, but it nonetheless remains an integral part of civil life in the western world. Jesus often spoke of the kingdom of God, but the question of what that means – whether that holy empire is to be of this world or not – remains as vital today as it was in the fourth century or in the sixteenth, precisely because faith and ethics, being and action, private and public life, prove impossible to separate in an enduring way.

VOICE OF THE TWENTIETH CENTURY

ELEANOR ROOSEVELT
1884-1962

Social activist. Adviser to her husband, President Franklin D. Roosevelt. Diplomat.

The citizens of a democracy must model themselves on the best and most unselfish life we have known … They may not all believe in Christ's divinity … but His life is important … If we once establish this human standard as a measure of success, the future of Democracy is secure.

Susan Cahill, editor, *Wise Women: Over Two Thousand Years of Spiritual Writing by Women* (New York: W.W. Norton and Co., 1996), 173.

KINGSHIP AND THE MARTYR'S CROWN

"I have been crucified with Christ; and it is no longer I who live, but Christ who lives in me...."

Galatians 2:20

To whom do Christians owe their allegiance in this world – Christ or Caesar? There was a river of blood running through the history of early Christianity, fed by the lives of martyrs who refused to reject Christ the King and submit to Caesar the emperor. For nearly three centuries after the Crucifixion of Jesus, Christians were forced to confront questions of faith which determined not only how they lived, but, in many instances, how they died.

CONSTANTINE, THE IRONY OF CHRISTIAN KINGSHIP

"Conquer by this!"

Eusebius,
Life of Constantine

On the eve of the Battle of Milvian Bridge in 312, Constantine I saw a cross inscribed "Conquer by this!" With Constantine's spiritual epiphany the Roman Empire passed into the hands of Christians. One of the world's great kingdoms was to be ruled in the name of a crucified King crowned with thorns. Christian kingship was riddled with contradiction and irony, but none was more perplexing than this – the suffering servant was said to have ascended the throne of royal power.

CHRIST THE KING, 1968.

Jean-Julien Bourgault, 1910-. Sculpture in wood. Canada. Musée de la civilisation [S1991-01494]. © SODART 2000. The struggle for the meaning of Christ the King has moved between interpreting him as Cosmic Emperor and as he who is crowned with humility and enthroned on the cross.

"All things were created through and for him. He is before all things, and in him all things hold together."

Colossians 1:15-19

In the first century, Jesus led a small group of disciples; by the fifth century, Christ had become the organizing principle and fundamental meaning of the cosmos. The human longing for order had found its end in Christ, *Logos* incarnate. The intellectual and spiritual implications of this are still felt.

In the first millennium, the sphere of Jesus' influence gradually expanded outward from the Jewish world he inhabited into the communities of Gentiles around the eastern Mediterranean. Eventually, his impact was felt throughout the whole of the Roman Empire. In the fifth century, through an encounter with Greek thought, Christian theologians extended that sphere one dimension further. Christ came to be understood as the *Logos* incarnate, the organizing principle of the cosmos, the being who imparts life and order to the universe, the reason for existence. All being in Creation, all animate life and inanimate things – past, present, and future – were created and sustained by Christ, the structure of being and the energy of the cosmos. The Cosmic Christ was a view of the divine that saw the glory of God in microscopic crystalline beauty and the movement of the heavens, indeed, in the whole order of Creation. The ability of God's Creation to inspire in the human mind consideration of the incomprehensible magnificence of God has influenced some of the monumental thoughts and achievements of western culture. As the eminent twentieth-century philosopher Alfred North Whitehead has noted, the roots of the modern scientific worldview are firmly planted in the soil of fifth-century Christian theology.

VOICE OF THE TWENTIETH CENTURY

ALBERT EINSTEIN

1879-1955

Theoretical physicist. Philosopher. Pacifist. Awarded Nobel Prize in Physics in 1921.

I want to know how God created this world. I am not interested in this or that phenomenon, in the spectrum of this or that element. I want to know [God's] thoughts, the rest are details.

Michael D. Robbins,
Tapestry of the Gods: Psychospiritual Transformation and the Seven Rays
(Rancho Santa Fe CA: University of the Seven Rays Publishing House, 1992), 822.

THE COSMIC CHRIST AND MODERN THOUGHT

"The religious concept of creation flows from a sense of wonder ... The scientific concept of creation encompasses no less a sense of wonder; we are awed by the ultimate simplicity and power of the creativity in physical nature...."

George Smoot,
Wrinkles in Time

A Christian Orthodox archbishop asked Stephen Hawking if there was any reasonable theory about non-barionic dark matter, which may be a way of explaining some of the tensions in the cosmos that seem to hold the universe together. Hawking responded, "You are an Eastern Orthodox monk so you must know the meaning of mystery." For the Christian East, this mystery at the centre of the cosmos is palpable and a source of wonder and comfort.

PENTECOST, 1985.

(top) Heiko Schlieper, 1931-. Icon. Canada. The Provincial Museum of Alberta [H85.1196.1]. The crowned figure emerging from the darkness at the base of the icon is the personification of the cosmos. All Creation has its origin and is illumined by the spirit of God.

SIDEREAL TIME, 1998-1999.

(below) Donald J. Forsythe, 1955-. Gouache, acrylic mediums, interference pigment, bronze leaf, plaster, burnish clay, charcoal ash over joss paper, and Bible pages on paper. United States of America. Collection Donald J. Forsythe. "Sidereal" represents the cosmic and orderly existence of God. Here Forsythe asks: "Do we seek God in community? With imperfect lenses? Through art? With scientific imaging? By gazing into the deep?"

> ## "Great art thou, O Lord, and greatly to be praised. ... Thou hast made us for thyself, and restless is our heart until it comes to rest in thee."
>
> Saint Augustine, *Confessions*

Christian thinkers realized the universality and uniqueness of Jesus' humanity contained fundamental insights which struck at the very core of the human experience of evil and suffering. They uncovered the curious paradox that in order to redeem human nature, God had to suffer and die at the hands of human beings.

It is significant to note that Jesus' most common name for himself in the Gospels is not "Son of God" or "Messiah," but rather "Son of Man." The choice of title is interesting. Jesus' followers see in their master the disclosure of divinity just as they see in his life and teaching the unveiling and recovery of human nature and what it means to live a deeply human life. After all, there was little about the basic facts of Jesus' life which suggested the magnificence traditionally attributed to divinity. He had been born to humble parents, had lived in a rural backwater of the Roman Empire, and had experienced personally and deeply the struggles of the human world – the hypocrisy of religious authorities, the faithlessness of friends, the savagery of imperial government. Jesus had taught about and lived in the midst of the human struggle. His path through this vale of tears ended in a brutal death which has become a ponderous spiritual riddle. How does one comprehend that he who came to redeem and restore human beings to the life of communing love died at the hands of the very ones he came to heal? The message of Jesus called the men and women of his day to recognize their deepest nature in a life of compassion expressed, not simply to one's friends and neighbours, but also to one's enemies and the stranger. For Jesus they were all Sons and Daughters of the same loving Father.

VOICE OF THE TWENTIETH CENTURY

MOTHER TERESA
1910-1997

Champion of the sick and impoverished of Calcutta. Leader of the Order of the Missionaries of Charity. Awarded Pope John XXIII Peace Prize in 1971, and Nobel Peace Prize in 1979.

"The spiritual poverty of the western world is much greater than the physical poverty of our people. You in the West have millions of people who suffer such terrible loneliness and emptiness. ... They know they need something more than money ... What they are missing really is a living relationship with God."

Mother Teresa, *Life in the Spirit: Reflections, Meditations, Prayers* (San Francisco: Harper & Row, 1983), 13-14.

Augustine's Path of Healing

"God loves us, such as we shall be, not such as we are."

Saint Augustine,
On the Trinity

While Saint Augustine focused upon the corruption of the human psyche after The Fall, he was also sensitive to the glory and sacrality of human existence. Original Sin obscured the reality of being created in God's image, but the human mind was still imprinted with "traces of divinity." As the link between God and Creation, Jesus was the model of what human nature had once been and should strive to become again.

Immaculate Mary and the Recovery of the Full Life

"Today the great mystery which has been announced from eternity … appears in the arms of Anne; Mary, the Maiden of God is prepared to be a dwelling of the King of Eternity who will renew our human nature."

Vespers for the
Maternity of Anne

A sensitive appreciation for Jesus' humanity requires an understanding of the Virgin Mary and the Immaculate Conception. For many Christian theologians, Mary was the "Second Eve," the impeccably pure woman who gave birth to the Messiah and thus erased the stain of Original Sin from the human psyche. For others, Mary was the mystical bridge between barrenness and abundance, between those who live without God and those who have discovered the fullness of life through Christ.

Resurrection: Rejoicing, 1946.

(top) Sir Stanley Spencer, 1891-1959. Oil on canvas. England. Beaverbrook Art Gallery [1959.209]. In Spencer's resurrection of the quick and the dead there is a vision of children rejoicing and dancing in ecstasy.

Saint Joseph and the Christ Child, 1912-1968.

(above) Plaster mould, polychrome painting. Canada. Musée de la civilisation [C1987-06537]. The Christ Child's humanity is plainly revealed as he walks alongside his human father, Joseph, and carries a cross, the symbol of his Passion, death, and Resurrection.

"He is the image of the invisible God."

Colossians 1:15

The view of Jesus as the True Image emerged in the debates on Christian iconography in the eighth and ninth centuries. In the image of Christ, human nature saw itself reflected and came to be understood as an icon of God, just as Christ was an icon of human nature.

Is it possible for the human mind to fathom the divine or the human hand to draw the image of God? In the eighth and ninth centuries, these questions absorbed Christian thinkers engaged in considering how – or even if – one should represent Christ in art. The second Commandment was a clear prohibition against any "graven images" of God. Jews and Muslims have long abided by this commandment and have avoided depictions of the divine. Christians, however, were faced with a problem particular to their faith: the divine was incarnate in Jesus of Nazareth. He was suckled as a child by his mother, walked the pathways of Galilee, sat at table with friends, taught those who cared to listen, and healed the suffering. God had become flesh. God had suffered and died on the cross. The footprints of the divine were part of the human world of daily life. This revelation brought fresh meaning to the ancient Biblical teaching that women and men were created "in the image and likeness of God." Jesus was the restoration of human nature and a revelation, an unveiling, of human nature healed of self-estrange-

ment. Through his life and gospel Jesus was a radiant example of how women and men, when fully themselves, were the image of God. By representing Christ in art, Christians engaged in consideration not only of the meaning of the divine, but, perhaps more importantly, of the meaning of the human.

VOICE OF THE TWENTIETH CENTURY

BASILEA SCHLINK
1904-present

In 1947, co-founded Evangelical Sisterhood of Mary in Darmstadt, Germany. Author of many books.

"Spend much of your time picturing Jesus. Meditate especially on Him as the Man of Sorrows. His suffering reveals all His beauty. Proclaim, declare, ever anew witness who your Bridegroom Jesus is, and your heart will be even more and more inspired to love Him."

Basilea Schlink, *My All for Him* (Minneapolis: Bethany House Publishers, 1971), 97.

JESUS, THE IMAGE OF GOD

"Because the one who by excellency of nature transcends all quantity and size and magnitude … has now … acquired a physical identity, do not hesitate any longer to draw pictures and to set forth, for all to see, him who has chosen to let himself be seen."

John of Damascus,
On the Images

For eighth-century iconoclasts, there was no thinker more dangerous than Saint John of Damascus (circa 675-circa 749). In Jesus of Nazareth, God had walked the earth as a man. Portraying Jesus in his humanity was a sacred duty, for it was only through his humanity, including his Passion, death, and Resurrection, that the meaning of his divinity became clear. For this he was branded by Christian iconoclasts a "traitorous worshipper of images" and "wronger of Jesus Christ."

THEOTOKOS AND CHILD (VLADIMIR, MOTHER OF GOD), 1985.

(top) Detail. Heiko Schlieper, 1931-. Icon. Canada. The Provincial Museum of Alberta [H85.1194.1]. The clarion call of Christian Orthodoxy was: all we know of God, we know through Jesus. The image of the child Jesus in his mother's arms became a compelling statement on the Incarnation of God.

CHRIST OF THE BREADLINES, 1950.

(above) Fritz Eichenberg, 1901-1990. Lithograph. United States of America. Yale University Library, Arts of the Book Collection. © Fritz Eichenberg Trust/VAGA/SODART 2000. In Dorothy Day's humble spirit, voluntary poverty, and, above all, ability to see the image of Christ in the vagrant begging for food, Eichenberg saw reflections of the deepest convictions of his soul.

"The power of the cross of Christ has filled the world."

Athanasius of Alexandria, died 373

Of all the images which engage and perplex the imagination, there are few more powerful than that of the crucified Christ. It is an image of God suffering and dying, of God's awesome power, wisdom, charity, and patience, and of God's incomprehensible love for humanity.

If one were asked to choose the symbol that has exerted the most profound influence on western civilization, would one be impelled to select the cross? There is almost certainly no emblem which has been as pervasive and as meaningful. In medieval Western Europe, a cultural world in many ways defined by the Church, the cross was *the* central symbol. Not surprisingly, a rich and elaborate theology developed around cruciform images. The cross was seen as an emblem of God's unfathomable power to conquer sin and call forth life from death itself; as a symbol of God's incomprehensible wisdom and mercy expressed through the Incarnation, Passion, Crucifixion, and Resurrection of Christ opening the door for redemption; and, above all, as the sign of God's infinite love for Creation. Along with, and perhaps because of, its deep and profound symbolic resonance for the medieval world, the cross also exerted a profound and immediate force upon the lives of those who believed in it. The cross became a kind of shorthand to invoke Christ's suffering and compassion for human suffering when afflictions called out for

healing and when other terrors of history threatened to unravel the life of the community. Regardless of one's religious affiliations, the symbol of the cross remains an awe inspiring subject of meditation and thought, focusing the attention of believers, and of those who anchor their confidence far outside the precincts of the church, upon wisdom, love, sacrifice, and the human condition.

VOICE OF THE TWENTIETH CENTURY

OSCAR ROMERO
1917-1980

Salvador-born Archbishop. Nominated for Nobel Peace Prize 1979. Killed during Mass.

"May my death ... be for the liberation of my people, and as a witness of hope in what is to come. You can tell them, if they succeed in killing me, that I pardon them ... A bishop will die, but the Church of God – the people – will never die."

Orientacion, 13 April 1980, quoted in James R. Brockman,
The Word Remains: A Life of Oscar Romero
(Maryknoll, NY: Orbis Books, 1982), 223.

THE TRUE CROSS AND THE IMPERIAL WORLD

Sing, my tongue, the glorious battle, / Sing the ending of the fray. Now above the cross, the trophy, / Sound the loud triumphant lay; Tell how Christ, the world's redeemer, / As a victim won the day.

Venantius Fortunatus, "Pange, lingua"

Following the conversion of the Roman Empire in 312, the sign of the cross took on the dimensions of a mystical talisman, radiating the awesome power of God. So forcibly did the symbol of the cross impress itself upon Constantine's mother, Helena, that she sought and, tradition says, recovered the True Cross. This symbol of the Empire's religious affiliations exerted a palpable power capable of routing enemies and protecting cities.

SILIQUA OF CONSTANTINE I (obverse) / PORTRAIT OF CONSTANTINE I (reverse), 336-337.

(above) Silver coin. Minted at Antioch. Collection T. Cheesman [RIC 105]. The relief portrait of the Emperor Constantine I on a siliqua (Roman silver coin), showing him in the attitude of praise, is an early illustration of his adoption of Christianity.

A VISION OF CHRIST'S BLOOD

"One cause of this barren blooming I attribute to a false system of education [of women], ... by men who ... have been more anxious to make them alluring mistresses than affectionate wives and rational mothers ...."

Mary Wollstonecraft, *A Vindication of the Rights of Woman*

In 1653 Marguerite Bourgeoys, a member of the Congregation of Notre-Dame de Troyes, sailed to New France. Several years earlier, at the age of twenty, she had received a mystical revelation. From that turning point, Marguerite knew that, like the Virgin Mary, she would pursue Jesus' teaching mission. Marguerite devoted herself to the education of young women because she was convinced that squandering a girl's potential was like spilling Christ's blood in vain.

CRUCIFIXION OF OUR LORD, 16TH CENTURY STYLE.

(below) Cretan School. Icon. Crete. Collection Heiko Schlieper. Mary the Mother of Jesus is shown with Mary Magdalene and another woman, while John is shown with the Roman centurion Longinus whom tradition identifies with the words "In truth this was a Son of God."

"Jesus came into Galilee, preaching the gospel of the kingdom of God ... "The time has come; the kingdom of God is upon you'."

Mark 1:14-15

"Gospel" (Greek *evangelion*) means "good news." Each of the four New Testament gospels, named for the traditionally proclaimed writers Matthew, Mark, Luke, and John, has a narrative of the teaching and deeds of Jesus, and identifies Jesus as the Promised One of Hebrew prophecy. Throughout twenty centuries of the Christian tradition the Gospels have been read in personal devotion, in worship services, and when Christians welcome children into the world, marry, and bury their loved ones. For many Christians, the Gospel story has been glimpsed primarily in prayer and worship and through iconography.

The icons of the twelve Great Feasts of the Church were painted by Heiko Schlieper (1931-).

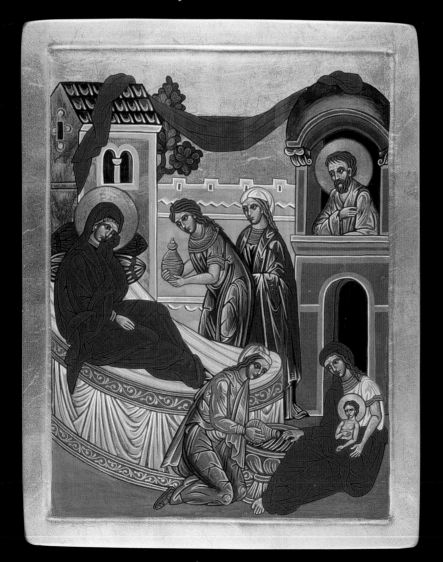

EXALTATION OF THE CROSS, 2000.
(top) Collection Heiko Schlieper. This feast, celebrated on 14 September, commemorates three historical occasions which involve the Cross on which Jesus was crucified: the legend of the finding of the Cross by Helena, Constantine's mother, the completion of the church of the Holy Sepulchre in Jerusalem, and the recovery of the Cross from the Persians in 629.

NATIVITY OF THE VIRGIN, 1999.
(left) Collection Heiko Schlieper. The Christian Church year begins in September with the Nativity of the Theotokos, 8 September being the first great feast day. Jesus' grandparents, Joachim and Anna, and the story of the birth of Jesus' mother Mary is found in the Protevangelium, a Christian apocryphal text probably dating from the end of the second century.

Entrance of the Theotokos into the Temple, 1993.

Collection Heiko Schlieper. The first feast of the Christmas season, 21 November, is based on the story of Mary's life in the Temple as a child found in the Protevangelium. Mary is shown as the fulfillment of the Covenant, a living temple, and as a type of the temple of the Holy Spirit of every human being.

Nativity of Our Lord, 1999.

Collection Heiko Schlieper. The feast celebrating the birth of Jesus focuses on the Incarnation of God in human form and depicts the birth accounts found in the Gospels of both Matthew and Luke. Along with the central story the icon also shows Joseph, betrothed to Mary, talking, as one tradition tells us, with his spiritual elder, seeking assurance that what has occurred is God's will.

Baptism of Our Lord, 1999.

Collection Heiko Schlieper. Theophany is the greatest of the winter feasts and honours the Baptism of Jesus, the prototype for every Christian, and the revelation of the Trinity. The feast day, 6 January, marks the beginning of Jesus' ministry and speaks of the blessing of all water and through that water, the blessed nature of the cosmos.

Meeting of Our Lord in the Temple, 1999.

This feast, known as early as the fourth century in Jerusalem, commemorates the fulfillment of the Law of Moses (Leviticus 12) forty days after Jesus' birth. The feast day is 2 February and the narrative speaks of the meeting of the Lord by Simeon and Anna, and the recitation of the beautiful *Nunc Dimittis*.

Annunciation, 1996.

Collection Heiko Schlieper. As early as the third century there is mention of the Annunciation as a feast in the Church. It is celebrated on 25 March, nine months before the birth of Jesus. The visitation of the Archangel Gabriel and Mary's openness to the message of the life she has conceived is depicted in the icon.

Entrance into Jerusalem, 1999.

Collection Heiko Schlieper. Falling one week before *Pascha* (Easter), this feast is popularly known as Palm Sunday. On this day the faithful hold palms, or branches of willows, to identify themselves with the people who greeted Jesus when he entered Jerusalem, a display of both political and eschatological significance as the beginning of the last week before his Crucifixion.

Ascension of Our Lord, 1999.

Collection Heiko Schlieper. Forty days after *Pascha*, this feast commemorates the end of the Resurrection appearances and the joyous "sitting down of Jesus Christ at the right hand of the Father." The Eastern Church follows the account in the Gospel of Luke.

Pentecost, 1999.

Fifty days after *Pascha*, this feast commemorates the account in the Acts of the Apostles of the descent of the Holy Spirit. The crowned figure emerging from the darkness is "Cosmos," a personification of illumined Creation, restored through its relationship to the Divine.

Transfiguration of Our Lord, 1999.

(right) The Provincial Museum of Alberta. Celebrated in Asia, probably by Armenians, as early as the fourth century, this feast was in wide use in the East by the year 1000. It is celebrated on 6 August and commemorates the Gospel event recorded in each of the synoptic Gospels. The East understands this event to speak of a transformed nature *(theosis)*, a glory shared by Moses and Elijah.

Dormition of the Virgin, 1999.

(left) Collection Heiko Schlieper. A feast day celebrated on 15 August commemorates the "falling asleep" (death) of Mary, the mother of Jesus. It draws attention to the sanctity of Mary's life. She is "the source of life laid in the grave and her tomb becomes a ladder to heaven." This feast is an apt conclusion to the cycle of the liturgical year, which began with Mary's birth.

"The desire of the flesh, the desire of the eyes, the pride in riches – comes not from the Father but from the world. And the world and its desire are passing away, but those who do the will of God live forever."

I John 2:15-17

In the fourth, fifth, and sixth centuries, Christ's invocation to his disciples to take up the cross and follow him became the mission for Christians who chose to abandon their worldly ambitions and walk in the footsteps of Jesus. They chose to live like Jesus – poor, chaste, and obedient.

When Jesus walked in Galilee and Jerusalem he was a man of singular simplicity. He showed no interest in wealth, position, or power, and at times seemed to reject them. While many of his close friends were women, he never married. Often in the Biblical narrative he described the seductiveness of the things and values that drive a wedge between those who have wealth and power and those who are on the margins of society. His life and call to his followers seem sharply at odds with conventional social ambition. In the first three centuries of Christian culture, there were a number of women and men who adopted Jesus' simplicity of life, a kind of voluntary poverty, and renounced the ambitions appropriate to their station in society. These early monastics, whether they withdrew to the desert or mountains or lived simply within the city or village, were a prophetic witness to dramatically different values. They were counterculture movements. In the fourth, fifth, and sixth centuries these largely diffuse movements began to take an organized shape. The monastic rules of poverty, chastity, and obedience, like the disci-

pline of athlete and artist, provided a structure which enabled women and men to pursue the kingdom of God in a life free of self-interest and open to God's grace. It is, as the monastic traditions have taught, in the profound depths of silence and stillness *(hesechia)* that one may hear the voice of God. This stillness is the heart of Christian monasticism.

VOICE OF THE TWENTIETH CENTURY

MOTHER MARIA SKOBTSOVA
1891-1945

Riga-born Russian Orthodox nun. Worked in Paris with Russian Orthodox Student Christian Movement. Sent to Ravensbruck by Nazis in 1943, where she demonstrated what it means to be human. Martyred just before end of World War II.

"At present monastics possess only one monastery, the whole wide world. The more we go out into the world, the more we give ourselves to the world, the less we are of the world. For the worldly do not give the world an offering of themselves."

Sergei Hackel, *Pearl of Great Price: The Life of Mother Maria Skobtsova, 1891-1945* (Crestwood NY: St Vladimir's Seminary Press, 1981), 27.

The Joy of Canada

O thornless rose of
ineffable beauty,
thou didst bud forth
on the border of paradise.
For through thine
unopened gate, the gate
was opened…
Wherefore we cry
unto thee:
Rejoice joy of Canada.

Akathist Hymn
for the *Theotokos
Joy of Canada*

Every year, New Ostrog, the
Orthodox Monastery of All
Saints of North America, in
Dewdney, British Columbia,
celebrates its feast day,
Theotokos, Joy of Canada.
The celebration speaks to the
faithful about the meaning
and purpose of the birth of
Jesus and calls them to identify
with the Theotokos ("Birth-
giver of God"), giving birth
to divine love in the world.
The Joy of Canada is focused
on the human vocation to
enter into cosuffering love
with all human beings.

Spiritual Struggle

"… If you wish to be per-
fect, go, sell your possessions, and give the money
to the poor, and you will
have treasure in heaven;
then come, follow me."

Matthew 19:21

The acknowledged founder
of Christian monasticism was
Saint Anthony the Great
(251?-356), although it is likely
that women's religious communities pre-date those of
men. Inspired by Jesus' imperative to abandon all worldly
possessions, Anthony jour-
neyed to the desert, where
he learned from other ascetics
before retiring from the
human community. In 305,
Anthony emerged to serve
as the spiritual leader for a
group of disciples. Similar
movements emerged across
Egypt and Syria.

Imago Pietatis
flanked by Saints,
circa 1428-1429.

Fra Angelico, circa 1387-1455.
Tempera and gold leaf on panel.
Italy. The Courtauld Gallery, London
[CL 10 A, B, C]. In an altarpiece,
of which this was the predella, the
image of the Crucifixion formed a
link to the bread and wine on the
altar. The woman saints include Mary
Magdalene and several virgin martyrs.

Batter my heart, three-person'd God, for you
As yet but knock, breathe, shine, and seek to mend;
...Take me to you, imprison me, for I,
Except you enthrall me, never shall be free,
Nor ever chaste, except you ravish me.

John Donne, Holy Sonnet XIV

In the twelfth century, the image of Christ as Bridegroom of the Soul emerged, which suggested the intimate relationship between the devout Christian and Jesus. Acceptance of Jesus was seen as an experience which would purge the soul, fill it with Christ's love, and mystically unite the faithful with God.

In the twelfth century, and particularly with the impetus of the Cistercian monastic movement, the ancient image of the Lover and the Beloved found in the Song of Songs in the Hebrew Bible emerged as a way of understanding the deeply personal relationship between Christ and the soul. Christ is the Bridegroom of the Soul. Christ woos the beloved and calls her to the garden of loving union. The rich cache of metaphors of romantic love, images that speak both of the single mindedness of the lover for the beloved and of the yearning of the beloved for the loved one, has come to characterize the heart of Christian spiritual life. However it came upon one, however one was grasped by the Lover, the experience would chase the darkness from one's soul, illuminate it with the light of Christ's presence, and vanquish the distance between God and the centre of one's being. The vision of Jesus as Bridegroom was a way of speaking about the intimate relationship between God, the Lover of the World, and Creation. It was a romantic view of the enduring presence of Christ as a spiritual companion united to his treasure at the very heart of the deepest human yearnings. At the centre of this image, wherever we find it, is the notion that Jesus, far from being an abstract and impersonal deity, unconnected to human affairs, is at the centre of the human heart illuminating the experience of the Beloved in the dailiness of life.

VOICE OF THE TWENTIETH CENTURY

AIMEE SEMPLE McPHERSON
1890-1944

Canadian-born evangelist and healer. Founded very successful Foursquare Gospel Movement in Los Angeles in 1918.

"Thou beautiful Bridegroom, Thou Prince of Peace, Thou Pearl of Great Price, Thou Rose of Sharon ... Oh, Jesus, to think that I shall live with thee forever and forever! ... I shall lean upon Thine arm, rest upon Thy bosom, sit upon Thy Throne, and praise Thee while the endless ages roll."

Aimee Semple McPherson, *This is That: Personal Experiences, Sermons, and Writings* (Los Angeles, CA, Echo Park Evangelistic Association, 1923), 636.

CHRIST-MYSTICISM OF BERNARD OF CLAIRVAUX

"... the reason for loving God is God Himself; and the measure of love due to Him is immeasurable ...."
Bernard of Clairvaux,
On Loving God

Saint Bernard of Clairvaux (1090-1153) embodied the thought and pieties of his age. He entered a monastery at twenty-two and practiced an asceticism of mind and body focused on the love of Christ and desire for union with the divine. The kiss of Jesus, a kiss of infinite compassion, enabled believers to join their nature to that of Jesus. It invited the devout into the chamber of his love, a sacred space, a bridal chamber.

THE DIVINE LOVER AND THE NEW MAGDALENE

"On this later day, a woman runs to grace who earlier ran to guilt. In the evening she seeks Christ who in the morning knew she had lost Adam ... She who had taken perfidy from paradise hastens to take faith from the sepulchre...."
Peter Chrysologus,
Sermon on Matthew 28:1

Perhaps the most dramatic image of the Divine Lover is in the stories of Saints Mary Magdalene and Mary of Egypt (5th century). Tradition portrays them led by God's love from a life of prostitution, abuse, and self-hatred through profound sorrow and repentance culminating in holiness and a life of loving service to the healing of others. These icons of repentance and models of the spiritual journey from self-hatred to divine love are the "New Eve."

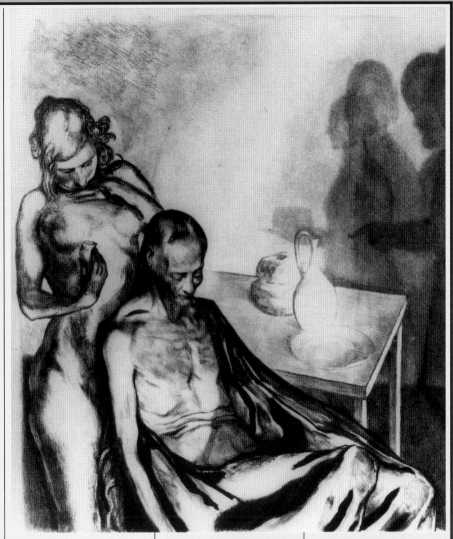

PRECIOUS OINTMENT, 1923.
(above) John Copley, 1875-1950. Lithograph. Scotland. Scottish National Gallery of Modern Art [GMA 245]. Mary of Magdalene is echoed in this novel depiction of the anointing of Jesus at the Last Supper. The artist speaks of the Incarnation and the recovery of Eden's purity through the use of the pristine human form.

CRUCIFIED CHRIST, 1960-1970.
(right) Vergour. Sculpture in wood. Musée de la civilisation [S1992-03272]. Since ancient times, the figure of Jesus, crowned with thorns and dying has been called the Bridegroom. Through taking death into Himself, God came again to be seen as wedded to human life.

> # "For whoever will understand the words of Christ plainly and in their full savour must study to conform all his [or her] life to his life."
>
> Thomas à Kempis, *Imitation of Christ*

The relationship Saint Francis of Assisi (1181/2-1226) had with Jesus was so intimate the historical and cultural distance between the two lives collapsed. Francis became the champion of all who felt the institutional church had lost sight of the true purpose of a Christian life – to conform to Christ's life.

The image of Jesus as the Divine and Human Model took vivid shape in one of the most profound stories of spiritual companionship, the late twelfth-century story of Jesus and Saint Francis of Assisi. The relationship between Francis and Christ was so intimate that their existences bled into one another. The Beloved became flesh as Francis sought not only to be joined to Christ in spiritual union, but also in corporeal union, as he struggled to conform the whole of his life to that of Jesus. Following Jesus, Francis abandoned his wealth, scorned the desires of the ego, and lived a life of utter simplicity. Just as Francis emulated Jesus in his simplicity of life and suffering, so too did he follow Jesus in his love for God's Creation. After centuries in which the Latin Church worked to expel nature worship from Europe, Francis ushered in a revivified sense of Creation and the wonders of the natural world as the playground of God's grace. Francis placed into sharp relief the distance between nominal Christians who tried to accommodate Jesus' teachings in much of their lives and those who have "put on Christ" and in so doing have taken delight in God's Creation and become servants of the most bereft in human society. Thus, though he did not intend it, Francis became a model for all those who have felt disillusioned with the Church and have sought to return to the most basic teaching of Christianity – the life of Christ.

VOICE OF THE TWENTIETH CENTURY

DOROTHY DAY
1897-1980

Social activist and author. Convert to Catholicism. Co-founder of monthly Catholic Worker *and* Catholic Worker Movement.

"I have said, sometimes flippantly, that the mass of bourgeois smug Christians who denied Christ in His poor made me turn to Communism, and that it was the Communists and working with them that made me turn to God...."

Dorothy Day, *Dorothy Day, Selected Writings: By Little and By Little,* edited by Robert Ellsberg (Maryknoll NY: Orbis Books, 1992), 7.

JESUS, THE DIVINE AND HUMAN MODEL

A DOUBLE LIFE: JESUS AND SAINT FRANCIS

"From now on, let no one make trouble for me; for I carry the marks of Jesus branded on my body."

Galatians 6:17

No single incident more dramatically revealed Saint Francis' identification with Christ than the miraculous happenings of September 1224. Saint Francis remained in solitude for forty days. At the end of his mountain retreat he was overcome by a vision. A seraph appeared and between its wings he beheld the crucified Christ. The appearance of the stigmata on Saint Francis' body speak of the profound affinity – of body, mind, and soul – between Francis and his Saviour.

THE HOLY FAMILY

"Let the little children come unto me; do not prevent them; for to them belongs the Kingdom of God."

Luke 18:15

Saint Francis of Assisi had proposed a cult of the Nativity, however, only after the Reformation were many images made to illustrate all the stages of Jesus' life. These included stories taken from the Bible, such as "Jesus before the Doctors in the Temple." Thus, the infant Jesus has touched many hearts. These images portray Jesus as the Divine and Human Model and unveil the mystery of divine grace at the heart of human experience.

SAINT CATHERINE OF SIENA,
MID 17TH CENTURY.
(left) Attributed to Francesco Cairo, 1607-1665. Oil on canvas mounted on wood. Italy. Musée du Périgord [Inv. B.15]. The stigmata were the sign that Catherine asked for and received during her vision. She received them on 1 April 1375 in front of the assembly in the Chapel of Santa Christina of Pisa.

SAINT CLARE WITH MONSTRANCE,
EARLY 16TH CENTURY.
(above) Sculpture in wood. Private Collection. Clare was so moved by the preaching of Francis of Assisi that she left the family home to join Francis. Later she became abbess for a community of women who lived according to Francis' monastic rule.

"Behold,
I make all things new."

Revelation 21:5

During the Renaissance, Europeans explored new regions of the world and the human mind. This led to a burgeoning of new ideas concerning Jesus and Christianity. As Renaissance thinkers breathed new life into the Gospels by returning to the Greek New Testament, they felt the spiritually redemptive message of Christ.

The Renaissance breathed new life into European civilization. The expansion of the human landscape through the European exploration of the New World was paralleled by expansion of the human mind and spirit through the re-discovery of the robust literature and philosophy of the ancient Greeks. This reinvigoration of European intellectual and cultural life gave birth to fresh ideas concerning Jesus, the Christian faith, and God's Creation. Jesus became the symbol of *Vita Nuova* (new life) and Christians throughout Europe found their faith and the natural world was suffused with the renewed radiance of Christ's being. The great Renaissance artists began to paint traditional religious subjects in strikingly new ways that accented the individual and the local landscape. Christian thinkers engaged sacred scripture with a new understanding of the thought and language of the ancient Greeks. Individuals everywhere became increasingly aware of the wondrous joys of the world that were offered to the receptive mind, heart, and soul. Renaissance art, literature, and

philosophy – so colourful, so alive – are testaments to the adventurous love of life and discovery that characterized the age. It is interesting to consider that the innovations of the Renaissance were not radically original creations, but were rooted in a Greek cultural and intellectual tradition centuries older than the Christian tradition itself. In order to recover the *Vita Nuova* of the present and particular world in which they lived, Renaissance thinkers returned to the deep cultural sources of the past.

VOICE OF THE TWENTIETH CENTURY

JEAN VANIER
1928-present

Theologian and philosopher. Officer of the Order of Canada. Founder of Fédération Internationale de l'Arche, dedicated to the spiritual and social development of the physically and mentally handicapped.

"With the Word becoming flesh"
Jesus makes all things new. The Word
became flesh precisely to be close to
the foolish and the powerless, to the
weak, to all those who do not have
the inner energy or power to walk up
the mountain of holiness.

Jean Vanier, *Jesus, the Gift of Love*
(London: Hodder and Stoughton Ltd.,1988), 146.

JESUS, THE UNIVERSAL MAN

JESUS AND THE RESTORATION OF HUMAN NATURE

"What else is the philosophy of Christ which He Himself calls a 'rebirth' [renascentia], than the restoration of [human] nature to the original goodness of its creation?"

Erasmus of Rotterdam,
Paracelsis

In Renaissance culture the revivification of a sense of humanity's grandeur was partly inspired by a sense that the expansion of the world and the mind was restoring humanity to its original state of wholeness. This rediscovery of the human world as the location of the sacred was intimately linked with the figure of Jesus, who became the paradigmatic symbol of all things valuable in the mind and spirit which were now being recovered.

THE LIGHT OF THE WORLD

"Now, when Christ enters any human heart, he bears with him a twofold light: first the light of conscience, which displays past sin, and afterwards the light of peace, the hope of salvation."

John Ruskin

Harking back to the Renaissance, William Holman Hunt depicted Jesus in an orchard at twilight knocking on a door overgrown by weeds. This was meant to suggest the inaccessibility of the human soul to the divine call in a materialistic age. Through the availability of high-quality prints, this image of Jesus as the "light of the world" became the icon of the emerging middle class – a personal Saviour unattached to the teachings of the churches.

LIGHT OF THE WORLD, 1851-1856.
(top) William Holman Hunt, 1827-1910. Poster. England. The Provincial Museum of Alberta. © Felix Rosenstiel's Widow and Son, Ltd. London.

NATIVITY, 1509-1511.
(left) Albrecht Dürer, 1471-1528. Woodcut. Germany. Private Collection. This woodcut from Dürer's "Small Passion" epitomizes his participation in the spiritual life of his day as well as his artistic and technical genius. The image is both powerful and serene.

CHRIST DRIVING THE MONEY CHANGERS FROM THE TEMPLE, 1635, IMPRESSION LATE 17TH OR EARLY 18TH CENTURY.
(above) Rembrandt van Rijn, 1606-1669. Etching. Netherlands. Christianson Collection. Like the fiery prophets of the Hebrew Bible, Jesus angrily denounces the avariciousness that prevented the poor from coming to the Temple.

"Jesus was the 'Mirror of the fatherly heart [of God], apart from whom we see nothing but a wrathful and terrible judge'."

Martin Luther, *Large Catechism*

The Reformation initiated arguably the most significant intellectual and cultural debate in western civilization. It often focused on Jesus' relation to the classical triad of Beauty, Truth, and Goodness. While most thinkers saw in Jesus the reflection of spiritual and intellectual Truth, there was little consensus on Beauty and Goodness.

When Martin Luther nailed his 95 Theses to the church door in Wittenburg and later refused to recant his criticisms of the Catholic Church, of which he sought to be a loyal servant, he initiated what is arguably the most significant intellectual and cultural debate in western civilization. Although Luther did not intend to cleave the church, his ideas spread rapidly. At the heart of the Reformation were questions about Jesus and his relationship to the classical triad of the Good, the True, and the Beautiful, represented in human terms respectively by the political, the intellectual and spiritual, and the aesthetic. While there was little disagreement about Jesus as a reflection of Truth, reformers were divided over the meaning of Christ as a reflection of Goodness and Beauty. Luther believed that Jesus' kingdom was not of this world and that one's duties as a citizen and as a Christian were separate. The other giant of the Reformation, John Calvin, believed that the ideal state was one in which faith and politics were inextricably linked. They disagreed about the aesthetic dimensions of Christianity as well: Luther asserted that art should be used to praise God, while Calvin feared the dangerous, potentially idolatrous, implications of Christian art. The Reformation changed the world by injecting into it new notions of the individual, of the authority of all that is taken as scripture free of the constraints of tradition and of the distinct spheres of religious life and secular authority.

VOICE OF THE TWENTIETH CENTURY

G. K. CHESTERTON
1874-1936

Poet, novelist, playwright, and social theorist. After conversion to Catholicism, wrote mainly on religious topics.

[The saint] will generally be found restoring the world to sanity by exaggerating whatever the world neglects … he is not what the people want, but rather what the people need …. Therefore it is the paradox of history that each generation is converted by the saint that contradicts it most.

G.K. Chesterton, in *First Things: A Monthly Journal of Religion and Public Life* 101 (March 2000), 23.

Jesus, the Mirror of the Eternal

Jesus, the Mirror in the Reformation

"… and they came and said to him, 'Teacher, … is it lawful to pay taxes to the emperor or not?'… Jesus said to them, 'Give to the emperor the things that are the emperor's, and to God the things that are God's'."

Mark 12:14, 17

The massive re-ordering of ideas, institutions, and civil society that constituted the Protestant Reformation found its most powerful exponent in Martin Luther. Disgusted by the decadence of the Catholic Church, Luther called for reforms based upon the example of Jesus, Mirror of the Eternal. Luther believed there should be separation of one's principles as a Christian and one's duties as a citizen. He also believed the arts should be used to praise God.

Jesus, the Mirror in the Catholic World

"… in Jesus Christ, as in a deep well, as in a vast ocean, we find a treasure of Being."

Luis de León,
Names of Christ, 1583

In the sixteenth century, Jesus was the transforming presence in the religious and cultural revival of both the Catholic Reformation and the Protestant Reformation. It was through seeing oneself in Jesus, argued Luis de León, Saint John of the Cross, and others, that the purpose and fulfillment of human life was glimpsed. The resolution of the tension between the knowledge of God and the love of God was found in Jesus, the Mirror of the Eternal.

Washing Peter's Feet (1922).

(above) Sir Stanley Spencer, 1891-1959. Oil on panel. England. Tullie House Museum and Art Gallery [CALMG:1936.56.1]. As a product of Spencer's experience of the horrors of World War I and his inclination to clothe the religious in homely attire, this image still speaks of the bonds Jesus has with humanity.

Expulsion from the Garden of Eden, 1869.

(left) Ford Madox Brown, 1821-1893. Pencil, ink, chalk, and wash. England. Beaverbrook Art Gallery [1990.10]. Brown drew upon his ability to create dramatic scenes for this stained-glass window design. Adam and Eve display the effects of The Fall, with the Tree of Life in the background.

Jesus with Five Wounds adored and mourned by an Angel, circa 1890.

(below) Sister Anastasia de la Visitation. Antependium. France. Musée des Pionniers et des Chanoinesses. Catholic piety has glimpsed in the Passion and death of Jesus both the meaning of human suffering and the triumph of the Eternal over the bondage of death.

Either we serve the Unconditional
Or some Hitlerian monster will supply
An iron convention to do evil by.

W.H. Auden, "Christmas 1940"

History is filled with atrocities and some use the name of Jesus to justify them, for example the Crusades, pogroms against the Jews, and strife in Northern Ireland. Christian thinkers throughout twenty centuries have confronted this profound existential crisis. Did Jesus come to bring a message of love or a sword?

It is a woeful reality that the history of Christianity, so intellectually rich and spiritually deep, includes in its legacy the taint of ignorance, hatred, and bloodshed. There have been the horrors of the Crusades, with their effect on both Orthodox Christian and Muslim communities, the periodic eruptions of anti-Semitism, and the occasionally bloody mixture of Christian faith with political and territorial ambitions. Many who claimed the Prince of Peace as Saviour slaughtered other Christians and both sides claimed God's divine authority to do so. There were a number of Christ's followers who asked: Is this what was taught by the best of Teachers? Had Jesus come not to bring peace, but a sword? A proliferation of new Christian movements during this period called upon the vision of Jesus as the Prince of Peace in order to re-emphasize the need to follow the counsels of Jesus absolutely and to reject unequivocally the path of violence. The image of Jesus as the Prince of Peace has inspired many who have sought to establish a peaceable world in which, in the words of the prophet Isaiah, the nations of the world "shall beat their swords into plowshares, and their spears into pruning hooks; nation shall not lift up sword against nation, neither shall they learn war any more" (Isaiah 2:4). As we leave the bloodiest century in human history and enter the third millennium, Christians and others alike confront the complex and often contradictory problems of establishing a peaceful world.

VOICE OF THE TWENTIETH CENTURY

HANNAH ARENDT

1906-1975

Political and social theorist.
Exile from Nazi Germany. Academic.

"The discoverer of the role of forgiveness in the realm of human affairs was Jesus of Nazareth … It is decisive in our context that Jesus maintains [that forgiveness] … must be mobilized by men toward each other before they can hope to be forgiven by God also."

Hannah Arendt, *The Human Condition*
(Chicago: University of Chicago Press, 1958), 238-239.

ASSEMBLÉE des QUAQUERS à Londres
A. Quaqueresse qui prêche

"YIELDEDNESS," ONE'S LIFE FOR PEACE

"... I say unto you,
do not resist an evildoer.
But if anyone strikes you
on the right cheek,
turn the other also...."
Matthew 5:39-40

In the "Radical Reformation" of the sixteenth and seventeenth centuries, Anabaptists were perhaps the most radical group. They asserted that proper Christian discipleship demanded a total "yieldedness" to the message and will of Christ, which necessarily implied rejection of all forms of violence. Beginning in 1525, Anabaptists across Europe began to be martyred for these views. The irony is morbid – the sixteenth-century groups who believed most ardently in peace were often the most brutally persecuted.

QUAKERS, FRIENDSHIP, AND PEACE

"...so it is strange that men, made after the image of God, should have so much degenerated, that they rather bear the image and nature of roaring lions ... and raging boars, than of rational creatures imbued with reason."
Robert Barclay, *Apology*

In the crucible of rapid change and social upheaval that characterized seventeenth-century England, George Fox (1624-1691), the founder and charismatic leader of the Quakers, boldly asserted that members of the Society of Friends would not participate in warfare because it was an act outside the perfection that Christ demanded of his followers. The Quaker spirit of pacifism and friendship was carried to America where it was manifested in equable relations with the native peoples.

QUAKER MEETING IN LONDON: A WOMAN SPEAKS, CIRCA 1736.
(top) Bernard Picart, 1673-1733. Engraving. France. The Provincial Museum of Alberta. In a Meeting for Worship, eighteenth-century Quakers waited in quietness for the guidance of the Holy Spirit before speaking. One of the Quaker's controversial beliefs was that ministry came through women as well as men.

SPIRITUAL MAZE WITH FOUR WELLS OF GRACE, 1785.
(above) Attributed to Henrich Otto. Watercolour on printed form on laid paper. Southeastern Pennsylvania. Rare Book Department, The Free Library of Pennsylvania [FLP 1057]. The text: "When I heard these words, I went on with joy... When I comprehended this, I had hope of being set straight... Now I have hopes of coming to the right path and way ...."

> # "This most beautiful system of the sun, planets, and comets was not to be attributed to some blind metaphysical necessity, but could only proceed from the counsel and dominion of an intelligent and powerful Being, who governs all things...."

Isaac Newton, *Mathematical Principles of Natural Philosophy*

Enlightenment thinkers like Voltaire and Diderot staged an assault upon Christianity. They savagely criticized the irrationality that characterized portions of the Christian worldview. Philosophers then dissected the New Testament and pored over historical documents to discover the "true Jesus." For them, Jesus' teachings had authority because they were intrinsically worthwhile.

During the Enlightenment, European thinkers began to question the Christian worldview that had been the heart of the continent for centuries. For most Enlightenment thinkers, the clarion call for the age was Immanuel Kant's imperative – *Sapere Aude* (Dare to know). Dare to know, dare to think for yourself, dare to reject those beliefs that seem incompatible with experience. Above all, dare to use the new understanding of reason to explore and think about your world. This dramatic challenge to the authority of the Church and the Christian tradition in Europe was accompanied by a new conception of the human being. Enlightenment thinkers tended to see humans primarily as creatures of reason, as individuals endowed with the capacity to grasp the whole of their experience and the world through the instrument of reason. Not surprisingly, this changed conception came, not solely from the secular *Philosophes* but also from within churches and led to a new under-

standing of Jesus as the Teacher of Common Sense. This vision of Jesus saw him not as some supernatural being descended from the heavens or as the Incarnation of God, but as a man of exceedingly sharp intellect. Jesus was a teacher, a moral instructor, and his teachings had validity not because they were a revelation of God to human beings, but because they were a rational guide for thought and behaviour.

VOICE OF THE TWENTIETH CENTURY

NORTHROP FRYE
1912-1991

Professor and editor. Internationally recognized literary critic. Companion of the Order of Canada. Ordained in United Church of Canada.

"The Gospels give us the life of Jesus in the form of myth ... Myth is neither historical nor anti-historical: it is counter-historical. Jesus is presented ... as a figure who drops into history from another dimension of reality, and thereby shows what the limitations of the historical perspective are."

Northrop Frye, *The Double Vision: Language and Meaning in Religion* (Toronto: United Church Publishing House, 1991), 16.

JESUS AND SOCRATES COMPARED

"This is the Spirit of truth, whom neither sees him nor knows him. You know him, because he abides with you, and he will be in you."

John 14:17

Jesus and Socrates both lived simply, were esteemed as excellent teachers, were regarded as traitors, and were executed for their beliefs. For some Enlightenment thinkers, the philosophy of Socrates was as liberating – as salvific – as the religion of Jesus. Others argued that Socrates' thought was beautiful, but Jesus' ideas and life were the very embodiment of God on this earth. Christian intellectuals have often noted that they were students of Socrates and disciples of Jesus.

THE RIGHTS OF MAN

"It is not enough to have overturned the throne; our concern is to erect upon its remains holy Equality and the sacred Rights of Man."

Robespierre, *Lettres à ses commettants*, 1792

The French Revolution of 1789 dissolved the monarchy, disestablished the Church, and proclaimed the advent of liberty, equality, and fraternity guaranteed by constitutional government. It was a watershed for the development of liberal democracy. Yet while it deposed the traditional Christian establishment, it opened the way for worship of collective human power with its ambiguous view of individual rights and national aspirations. This struggle to hold these competing values together still dominates our political life.

RICH ROBINSON, BARON ROBERT, LORD PRIMATE OF ALL IRELAND *(obverse)*/ OBSERVATORY *(reverse)*, 1789.

(left) Medallion. Ireland. Collection T. Cheesman. Richard Robinson (1709-1794), Lord Archbishop of Armagh and Primate of All Ireland (1765-1794), was an important supporter of the development of modern astronomy and founded Armagh Observatory in 1790.

DEATH OF SOCRATES, 1762.

(below) Jacques-Philippe-Joseph de Saint-Quentin, 1738-circa 1780. Oil on canvas. France. École nationale supérieure des Beaux-Arts, Paris [PRP 10]. Socrates and Jesus served as tap-roots of Western culture, buried deep in the soil of Athens and Jerusalem. Both encouraged self knowledge and were magnificent teachers. Both were sentenced for their teaching and executed.

> "The truly divine element [in Jesus] is the glorious clearness to which the great idea he came to exhibit attained in his soul: that all that is finite requires a higher mediation to be in accord with the Deity ...."
>
> Friedrich Schleiermacher, *On Religion: Speeches to its Cultured Despisers*

In the eighteenth and nineteenth centuries, Europeans attempted to liberate Jesus from the prison of reason Enlightenment thinkers had erected. The Romantics saw Jesus as the locus of the vital relationship between human nature and nature, the conscious mind and unconscious intuition. This Jesus was the artistic impulse made flesh.

In the eighteenth and nineteenth centuries, the image of Jesus as the Teacher of Common Sense was challenged by poets, painters, and intellectuals of the human spirit. They saw in the Gospel accounts of Jesus' life, teaching, and actions – whether miracles, parables, his rich repartee or simple touching of the estranged person – a rich symbolism and creative flair. To the artists and philosophers of this period, the suggestion that Jesus was little more than a moral teacher seemed preposterous. Many of the Romantic poets, artists, philosophers, and theologians sought to free Jesus from the prison of reason and restore to Jesus, and through him to our understanding of human nature, the miracle and mystery of being. This new image of Jesus envisioned him as the Poet of the Spirit. Jesus embodied the creativity which knits together all the threads of the human soul. He was the Muse who inspired poets and painters, the artistic impulse made flesh. Jesus wove together the conscious mind and the unconscious intuition, the depth of the self and the wonder of the world, the human being and the glory of the natural world. When we consider the remarkable tradition of Christian artists – from the unnamed women artists of the early Church to Phoebe Anna Traquair, from Gregory of Nyssa to Dante and William Blake, from Hildegard von Bingen to Bach and Lina Sandel, to name just a few – we also ponder the depth and range of the human spirit's engagement with what in the nineteenth century came to be called the Poet of the Spirit.

VOICE OF THE TWENTIETH CENTURY

ANNA AKHMATOVA
1889-1966

Born in Odessa, she studied in Kiev before moving to St Petersburg. Prolific poet officially silenced several times by Soviet government.

Anno Domini (1922)
To earthly solace, heart, be not a prey,
To wife and home do not attach yourself,
Take the bread out of your child's mouth,
And to a stranger give the bread away.
Become the humblest servant to the man
Who was your blackest enemy,...
And do not ask God for anything.

Anna Akhmatova, *Way Of All The Earth*, translated by D.M. Thomas (Athens OH: Ohio University Press, 1979), 54.

THE EVERLASTING GOSPEL

Jesus and his Apostles and his Disciples were all Artists ... The Old and New Testaments are the Great Code of Art. Art is the Tree of Life. GOD is Jesus. Science is the Tree of Death.

William Blake,
The Laocoon

William Blake criticized the Enlightenment understanding of Jesus. In *The Everlasting Gospel*, Blake presents Jesus not as a moral theorizer or a prodigious philosopher, but as the very embodiment of the "poetic," as a supremely creative being above rigid dogma, harsh logic, and morality. Jesus explodes from the pages of Blake's poetry with his fierce apocalyptic view. For Blake, Jesus becomes a symbol of *being*, of the vital and non-dualistic relationship between divinity and humanity.

DOSTOEVSKY AND THE RAISING OF LAZARUS

"... Martha, the sister of the dead man, said to him, 'Lord, already there is a stench because he has been dead four days.' ... [Jesus] cried with a loud voice, 'Lazarus, come out!' The dead man came out ...."

John 11:39, 43-44

Whereas Enlightenment thinkers had tended to discount miracles, many Romantic and post-Romantic artists saw them as a truth with profound significance. This is forcibly expressed in *Crime and Punishment* when Sonia reads to Raskolnikov the tale of Jesus raising Lazarus from the dead. The story of Lazarus' resurrection leads Raskolnikov to the possibility of cleansing and rebirth, a restoration of his spirit and a new joy in the world, from which he has been estranged.

THE COMPLAINT AND THE CONSOLATION, OR, NIGHT THOUGHTS BY EDWARD YOUNG, 1797.

(left) William Blake, illustrator, 1757-1827). Watercolours and engravings. England. Peel Special Collections Library, University of Alberta. Blake's 537 watercolour designs and 43 engravings for this poem were his largest pictorial work. Young's imagery, transformed by Blake's visionary imagination, shine as an illuminated serial fresco of irony, comedy, and prophecy.

THE FOUR GOSPELS OF THE LORD JESUS CHRIST, ACCORDING TO THE AUTHORIZED VERSION OF KING JAMES I, 1931.

(above) Eric Gill, illustrator, 1882-1940. Engravings. England. Peel Special Collections Library, University of Alberta. Gill was a craftsman, engraver, type designer, sculptor, philosopher, convert to Catholicism, and poet of the spirit. His most famous type, Perpetua, named for the second century martyr, is used in this book.

JESUS AND INQUISITOR, ENCOUNTER. CIRCA 1942.

(below) Fritz Eichenberg, 1901-1990. Sketch. United States of America. Yale University Library, Arts of the Book Collection. © Fritz Eichenberg Trust/VAGA/SODART 2000. The encounter between the radiant Christ and the feeble Grand Inquisitor expresses the sharp contrast between the mystery and profound meaning of Jesus and the occasional defilement and degradation of his spirit in those who claim his name.

"Man is born free, and he is everywhere in chains."

Jean-Jacques Rousseau,
The Social Contract

In the nineteenth and twentieth centuries the explanation of Jesus' Crucifixion was that Jesus had become Incarnate to free anyone trapped in bondage, to give humanity back its dignity. The vision of Christ as Liberator still resounds in the clarion call of the American civil rights movement, "Let freedom ring."

There was something in the glowing images of Christ presented by Enlightenment thinkers and Romantic poets that struck some people in the nineteenth and twentieth centuries as incongruous. If Jesus' true significance was as a paragon of rational discourse or an artistic genius, why had he been crucified as a common criminal? Why had such an eminently appealing figure been flogged, mocked, and finally nailed to a cross? One of the remarkable and compelling responses to these questions was the image of Jesus, the Liberator. Jesus had driven the money-changers out of the temple. Throughout the Gospels we see him consistently siding with the dispossessed, alienated, and estranged – tax collectors, prostitutes, lepers, and the rich young ruler. In the nineteenth and twentieth centuries thinkers both inside and outside the Church drew into the foreground of consideration the ancient teaching which saw Jesus as a healer endeavouring to release women and men from all forms of bondage – mental, spiritual, physical, social, and political. He responded with blessings to all who sought him out. His blessing affirmed

the dignity of the person and the struggle to become whole. Like few others in the history of human compassion Jesus affirmed human dignity free of regard for one's station in life, one's religious position or how one was viewed by society. It is the liberty Jesus seemed to embody that eventually ran afoul of political and social institutions and led to his execution.

VOICE OF THE TWENTIETH CENTURY

DOROTHY SAYERS
1893-1957
Author. Christian apologist.

"Perhaps it is no wonder that the women were first at the Cradle and last at the Cross. They had never known a man ... who took their questions and arguments seriously; who never mapped out their sphere for them ... who took them as he found them and was completely unself-conscious."

Dorothy Sayers, *Unpopular Opinions*
(London: V. Gollancz, 1951), 121-122.

AMAZING GRACE ABOARD THE SLAVE SHIP

"John Newton, Clerk, once an infidel and libertine … was, by the rich mercy of our Lord and Saviour Jesus Christ, preserved, restored, pardoned, and appointed to preach the faith he had long laboured to destroy."
Inscription on John Newton's Tombstone

On 10 May 1748, as his ship was tossed about, John Newton implored God for deliverance from the storm. That deliverance profoundly affected his life. Once a commander of a slave ship, Newton dedicated his life to the abolitionist movement. In 1807, shortly before his death, the English government formally ended the practice of slave trading. Newton's passage from darkness to light has been immortalized in the lines of his most famous hymn, "Amazing Grace."

JESUS, LIBERATOR OF SLAVES

"… one day the South will know that when the disinherited children of God sat down at lunch counters, they were in fact standing up for what is best in the American dream and for the most sacred values in our Judeo-Christian heritage …."
Martin Luther King, Jr,
Letter from the Birmingham Jail

Martin Luther King, Jr (1929-1968) was inspired by a vision of radical obedience to Christ and discipleship. King found in Holy Scripture, especially the Sermon on the Mount, the supreme expression of love for one's brothers and sisters which transcends violence and

hatred. This love was embodied in the practice of non-violent resistance. The price of King's discipleship was high. He was assassinated, but his vision of freedom and equality for all peoples lives on.

GANDHI'S JESUS

"When I read the Sermon on the Mount, especially such passages as 'Resist not evil,' I was simply over-joyed. … The gentle figure of Christ, so patient, so kind, so loving, so full of forgiveness … was a beautiful example, I thought, of the perfect man."
Mohandas Gandhi

Leo Tolstoy wrote a letter asserting his belief in "the teaching of love," which he found most completely embodied in the message of Christ. The recipient of the letter was Gandhi, and the idea became reality in Gandhi's campaign of non-violence to oppose British rule in India. Inspired by the Sermon on the Mount, in particular, Gandhi used the most radical of tools – non-aggression – to stymie and ultimately overthrow the system of British colonial rule.

GANDHI IN PRISON.
(above) Photograph. India. Gandhi Memorial Museum, Madurai, India. Mohandas Gandhi spent twenty years in Africa where he worked against racial prejudice before he returned to India to lead the movement for civil disobedience which culminated in the end of British colonial rule. He was jailed for conspiracy on a number of occasions and was assassinated in Delhi on 30 January 1948.

SHOW SOLIDARNOŚĆ WITH POLISH PEOPLE, 1981.
(above) E. Chruścicki. Poster. Poland. Collection Lillian Petroff. Portraying the events of the anticommunist struggle in Poland through such Christian symbolism as crosses, anchors, and radiant light illustrates the moral authority the Catholic Church retained throughout those dark days.

AFRICANS OF THE SLAVE BARK "WILDFIRE" BROUGHT INTO KEY WEST ON APRIL 30, 1860.
(above) Woodcut from daguerreotype in *Harper's Weekly: A Journal of Civilization*, 2 June 1860. United States of America. University of Alberta Library. The ship left Africa with 600 slaves, 90 of whom died on the voyage. Many abolitionists believed the inherent dignity of people made in the likeness of God necessitated the end of American slavery.

JOHN BROWN REMAINED A FULL WINTER IN CANADA, DRILLING NEGROES FOR HIS COMING RAID ON HARPERS FERRY, *from series "Legend of John Brown,"* 1977.
(centre) Jacob Lawrence, 1917-2000. Screenprint on wove paper. United States of America. Courtesy of the Artist and The Detroit Institute of Arts, Founders Society Purchase, Commissioned by Founders Society Detroit Institute of Arts, 1978 [F1983.18.17]. John Brown (1800-1859) believed Christianity required him to act against slavery, because it was an affront to freedom and human dignity. In 1859 he led an unsuccessful raid on the armory at Harper's Ferry.

"The uniqueness of Christ as the historical revealer, as the Word made flesh, and the mystery of Calvary [compel the affirmation that] God reveals himself in history, outside the Church as well as in it."

Archbishop Nathan Söderblom, Gifford Lectures, 1931

Christian missionaries have established schools, healed the sick, and comforted the suffering everywhere. They have also participated in the colonial impulse that has, at times, brutalized other cultures. However, it is through his ability to fascinate the mind and inspire the spirit that Jesus has transformed the spiritual landscape.

In the twentieth century, as technological innovations, immigration, and education obliterated the borders separating cultures, a new vision of Jesus emerged – the Man Who Belongs to the World. For centuries, Christian evangelists have brought the Christian message to people in every corner of the globe. These missionaries have established educational programs, fed the starving, and comforted the suffering. Some missionaries have also participated in imperial and colonial movements that have brought both the gifts and diseases of the European West, and with them, the transformation and brutalization of cultures. It is one of the great curiosities of the colonial period in European and American society that Christian missionaries made the teachings of Jesus accessible to virtually the entire world and he has been used to throw off the bondage of colonialism. We also see in the modern world how many of these cultures have woven Jesus into the pattern of their culture, regardless of whether they accept Western civilization or the Church as a harbinger of a better life or Jesus

as Saviour. As we look back over the twenty centuries of Christian culture, we are reminded that Jesus has shaped and reshaped more than one civilization and many cultures, and, now, as the eminent historian of Christian ideas Jaroslav Pelikan has said, "he belongs to the world."

VOICE OF THE TWENTIETH CENTURY

MOHANDAS KARAMCHAND GANDHI
1869-1948

Campaigner for Indian independence and moral reform. Proponent of civil disobedience.

"What, then, does Jesus mean to me? To me, He was one of the greatest teachers humanity ever had. To His believers, He was God's only begotten son. Could the fact that I do or do not accept this belief make Jesus have any more or less influence on my life?"

The Book of Jesus: A Treasury of the Greatest Stories and Writings about Christ, edited by Calvin Miller (New York: Simon and Schuster, 1996), 57.

SUFFER LITTLE CHILDREN TO COME UNTO ME, 1874, 1934-1935.
(facing page) Sir Edward Coley Burne-Jones, 1833-1898. Hand-woven tapestry. England. Church of Saint Andrew and Saint Paul, Montreal. Though this scriptural event occurs in three of the four Gospels, portrayal of the Christian symbolism of innocence and trust inherent in the narrative is unusual in art.

suffer little children to come unto me

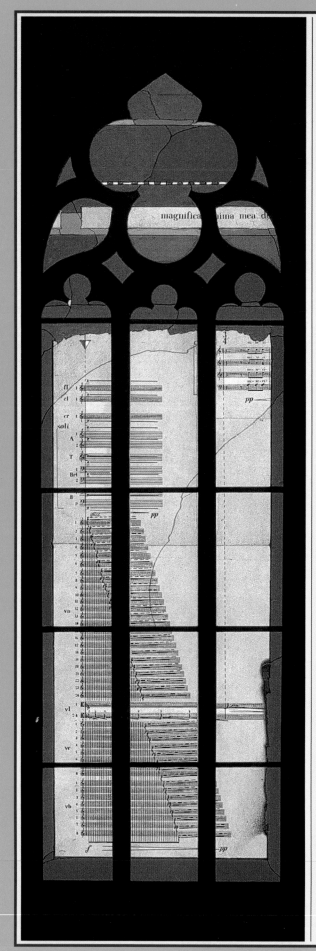

SOUNDSCAPE 1

JESUS THE JEW

Jesus was born into a people buffeted by war, political crisis, exile, and oppression. Hebrew scriptures give us a glimpse of this people's desperate longing for a transformation of their world. They called for a wise teacher, the return of the prophet Elijah, and a saviour to deliver the people of Israel from their oppressors. The Jews cried out for a rabbi, a prophet, and a Messiah. Did the Jewish community express these cries musically? Undoubtedly they did, but unfortunately, we cannot hear those voices. We have no recordings, no extant notated music. This was an oral tradition, inevitably evolving over time. Literary references describe music among the Jewish people, but assumptions about how this music sounded are only conjecture. We cannot listen to Jesus' own music. Instead, we can hear echoes of Jesus' words, the resonance of the Hebrew people's deepest longings, and the articulation of questions surrounding Jesus' identity. We can respond to musical voices from the ninth to the twentieth centuries - composers, poets, and performers interpreting Jewish culture and Jesus' place in it. The conversation about Jesus continues in musical creations of our own day.

SOUNDSCAPE 2

TURNING POINT OF HISTORY, LIGHT OF THE GENTILES, KING OF KINGS, COSMIC CHRIST, SON OF MAN, TRUE IMAGE

This music explores Jesus' dual nature. Throughout millennia, Christians have celebrated the paradoxes of Jesus' divinity and humanity: the Jew of humble birth became the Light of the Gentiles, the King of Kings consorted with the very least of his brethren, the Creator died to redeem his Creation, and the eternal *Logos* intervened in human history, redirecting its course. Most remarkably of all, the Son of Man born to a woman was also God Incarnate, his True Image. At different times and in disparate cultures, believers have related strongly to each of these likenesses; they have seen in Jesus the fulfillment of their particular needs and longings. This section presents some of the ways various cultures and eras reflect these images in music.

MUSIC WINDOW, 1983.
Johannes Schreiter, 1930-. Enamelled and stained glass window. Schreiter's design includes excerpts of works that have revolutionized music in the last century or been played in church-sponsored recitals. Penderecki's *Magnificat*, a blue spiral notation by American composer John Cage signifying an experimental type of eternal melody, and a voice chart by Italian Sylvano Bussotti are juxtaposed with a rough handwritten scrap of Gregorian chant from the days when musical notation was also experimental. A U-shaped bracket at the extreme top of one design possibly represents Schreiter's conviction that of all human achievements, music in particular can be given back to God as a sublime gift.

SOUNDSCAPE 3

CHRIST CRUCIFIED, MONK WHO RULES THE WORLD, BRIDEGROOM OF THE SOUL, DIVINE AND HUMAN MODEL, UNIVERSAL MAN, AND MIRROR OF THE ETERNAL

The images in this section are all inversions of conventional images. The cross, an instrument for humiliation and torture, becomes the place of triumph and an instrument for restoring human dignity. The monastic tradition conquers the world by denying it and the soul is fulfilled when its lover takes on flesh. Voices of dumb animals express profound praise; human nature is recovered through the One who shares the divine nature; and by gazing on Jesus the believer sees both God the Father, and himself or herself. Many of the musical examples in this section also seem incongruous. Popular love song styles speak of mystical union with God, a cantata celebrates the attributes of animals, and the solitary voice of an old man singing becomes the occasion for a superimposed orchestral composition. "I am not ashamed to confess publicly that next to theology there is no art which is equal to that of music." This, from the pen of Martin Luther (1483-1546) in 1530, accounts in part for the flourishing of Lutheran congregational hymnody and sacred service music. It also suggests that music has a unique capacity to transform simple human expression and experience into contemplation of the divine.

SOUNDSCAPE 4

PRINCE OF PEACE, POET OF THE SPIRIT, LIBERATOR, TEACHER OF COMMON SENSE, AND MAN WHO BELONGS TO THE WORLD

Music often functions as background in our lives: ever-present, but not the centre of attention. If you move music to the fore-ground, it can be a means of exploring images of Jesus. Eighty percent of the music in this area was written in the twentieth century - a concrete symbol of the continuing meaning these images carry in the conversation around Jesus. The variety of musical styles represents contrasting voices engaging in this conversation. Some of these voices are familiar, others may seem foreign or even inappropriate. But they all enhance our contemplation of Jesus as Prince of Peace, Poet of the Spirit, Liberator, Teacher of Common Sense, and Man Who Belongs to the World.

SOUNDSCAPE 5

JESUS OF THE GOSPEL

The life of Jesus of the Gospels shapes the worship of Christian communities everywhere. This life is the guide and pattern celebrated in song and sermon. It orders the cycle of the Church year that commemorates this life and ministry from Nativity to Ascension, and it informs sacramental and liturgical symbol and imagery. Jesus' life as a human being begins, as it does with all of us, in his mother's womb. Gabriel's greeting: "Hail Mary, full of grace, the Lord is with you" introduces the Annunciation, the first celebration of the Incarnation that culminates in Jesus' death, Resurrection, and Ascension celebrated during the Easter season. Within many traditions, this passage from life to death to life, the complete Christian cycle, is celebrated every Sunday of the year. The music chosen for this section relates to the icons and biblical passages of the exhibition, either as music that is proper to a specific day or celebration depicted in an icon, or as music that invokes these images from the unvarying texts that make up the framework of a given liturgy, including texts such as the Nicene Creed or the Lord's Prayer. Because religious traditions such as Christian Byzantine rites and Jewish worship use unaccompanied human voices in the context of worship, all of the selections presented in this section are a capella - not accompanied by instruments.

SOUNDSCAPE 6

ILLUMINED COSMOS OF JOHANNES SCHREITER

"Holy, holy, holy, Lord God of hosts, Heaven and earth are full of thy glory. Hosanna in the highest. Blessed is he that cometh in the name of the Lord. Hosanna in the highest."

These proclamations of worship, derived from Isaiah 6:3, are familiar to Christians of nearly every tradition. Clement of Rome, who died circa 104, noted their use at the dawn of the Church. Visualize the powerful, startling imagery of Isaiah's vision. The Lord sits upon a throne elevated on high, while above, seraphim cry out to one another: "Holy, holy, holy, is the Lord of hosts: the whole earth is full of his glory." Stained-glass images invite us to join in this hymn of praise. We are called to celebrate the presence of *Logos* in science, literature, music, and art, and to see heaven and earth full of the glory of God. The stained-glass artist Johannes Schreiter has expressed the sacred through representations of the unconventional. In a similar way, the richness and diversity of musical expression may compel us, as listeners, to recognize the myriad resources which people bring to their worship of God. No one mode of praise can adequately represent everyone; indeed, worship is an expression of adoration which, at its most profound and personal, transcends words. All the music here is drawn from the twentieth century. Each work is a particular treatment of Isaiah's hymn which Christians call the Sanctus.

FURTHER READING

PELIKAN, Jaroslav. *Jesus Through the Centuries: His Place in the History of Culture* (New Haven CT: Yale University Press, 1985) and *The Illustrated Jesus Through the Centuries* (New Haven CT: Yale University Press, 1997).

ALTIZER, Thomas J.J. *The Contemporary Jesus* (Albany NY: State University of New York Press, 1997).

BARROIS, Georges Augustin. *Jesus Christ and the Temple* (Crestwood NY: St. Vladimir's Seminary Press, 1980).

BERGMAN, Susan, ed. *Martyrs* (San Francisco CA: HarperSanFrancisco, 1996).

BORG, Marcus J. Jesus, *A New Vision: Spirit, Culture, and the Life of Discipleship* (San Francisco CA: Harper & Row, 1987).

BORG, Marcus J., ed. *Jesus at 2000* (Boulder CO: Westview Press, 1997).

BORNSTEIN, Daniel and RUS-CONI, Roberto, eds. *Women and Religion in Medieval and Renaissance Italy* (Chicago IL: University of Chicago Press, 1996).

BORST, Arno. *The Ordering of Time: From the Ancient Computus to the Modern Computer* (Cambridge UK: Polity Press in association with Blackwell, 1993).

BRIA, Ion, ed. *Jesus Christ — the Life of the World: An Orthodox Contribution to the Vancouver Theme* (Geneva, Switzerland: World Council of Churches, 1982).

BUECHNER, Frederick. *The Faces of Jesus* (Croton-on-Hudson NY: Riverside Publishers, 1974).

BULL, Josiah. *John Newton of Olney and St. Mary Woolnoth: An Autobiography and Narrative, Compiled Chiefly from His Diary and Other Unpublished Documents* (London UK: Religious Tract Society, 1868).

BUTLER, John Francis. *Christianity in Asia and America after A.D. 1500* (Leiden, Netherlands: E.J. Brill, 1979).

CARSON, Clayborne and HOLLO-RAN, Peter, eds. *A Knock at Midnight: Inspiration from the Great Sermons of Reverend Martin Luther King, Jr.* (New York NY: IPM Intellectual Properties Management, Inc. in association with Warner Books, 1998).

COOPER, Michael, S.J. *Rodrigues the Interpreter: An Early Jesuit in Japan and China* (New York NY: Weatherhill, 1974).

CRAGG, Kenneth. *Jesus and the Muslim: An Exploration* (Oxford UK: Oneworld Publications, 1999).

CROSSAN, John Dominic. *The Historical Jesus: The Life of a Mediterranean Jewish Peasant* (New York NY: HarperCollins, 1991).

CROSSAN, John Dominic. *Jesus: A Revolutionary Biography* (San Francisco CA: HarperSanFrancisco, 1994).

DOUMERGUE, Émile. *Iconographie Calvinienne* (Lausanne: Georges Bridel & Cie Éditeurs, 1909).

ENDO, Shusaku. *A Life of Jesus* (New York NY: Paulist Press, 1978).

ERB, Peter C., ed. *Pietists: Selected Writings* (New York NY: Paulist Press, 1983).

FITCHETT, W.H. *Wesley and His Century: A Study in Spiritual Forces* (Toronto ON: William Briggs, 1908).

FOX, George. *The Journal of George Fox* (Cambridge UK: Cambridge University Press, 1911).

FRANCIS OF ASSISI, Saint and CLARE OF ASSISI, Saint. *Francis and Clare: The Complete Works* (New York NY: Paulist Press, 1982).

GANDHI, Mahatma K. *The Story of My Experiments with Truth* (Ahmedabad, India: Navajivan Publishing House, 1927-1929).

_____. *Hind Swaraj and Other Writings* (Cambridge UK: Cambridge University Press, 1997).

GREGORIOS, Paulos Mar. *Cosmic Man: The Divine Presence: The Theology of St. Gregory of Nyssa (ca 330 to 395 A.D.)* (New Delhi, India: Sophia Publications, 1980).

GROESCHEL, Benedict J. *Spiritual Passages: The Psychology of Spiritual Development "for those who seek"* (New York NY: Crossroad Publishing Company, 1983).

HELLWIG, Monika K. *Jesus, the Compassion of God: New Perspectives on the Tradition of Christianity* (Wilmington DE: M. Glazier, 1983).

JEANROND, Werner G. and THEOBALD, Christoph, eds. *Who Do You say That I Am?* (London UK: SCM Press, 1997).

JULIAN, of Norwich. *Showings* (New York NY: Paulist Press, 1978).

KIENZLE, Beverly Mayne and WALKER, Pamela J., eds. *Women Preachers and Prophets Through Two Millennia of Christianity* (Berkeley CA: University of California Press, 1998).

KINTZ, Linda. *Between Jesus and the Market: The Emotions That Matter in Right-Wing America* (Durham NC: Duke University Press, 1997).

MCDANNELL, Colleen. *Material Christianity: Religion and Popular Culture in America* (New Haven CT: Yale University Press, 1995).

MEADE, Catherine M., C.S.J. *My Nature is Fire: Saint Catherine of Siena* (New York NY: Alba House, 1991).

MILLER, Calvin. *The Book of Jesus* (New York: Simon and Schuster, 1996).

NELLAS, Panayiotis. *Deification in Christ: Orthodox Perspectives on the Nature of the Human Person* (Crestwood NY: St Vladimir's Seminary Press, 1987).

NEWTON, John. *The Works of the Rev. John Newton, Late Rector of the United Parishes of St Mary Woolnoth and St Mary Woolchurch-Haw, Lombard Street, London* (Edinburgh UK: Printed at the University Press for Thomas Nelson and Peter Brown, 1835).

NORRIS, Kathleen. *Amazing Grace: A Vocabulary of Faith* (New York NY: Riverhead Books, 1998).

PELIKAN, Jaroslav. *Mary Through the Centuries: Her Place in the History of Culture* (New Haven CT: Yale University Press, 1996).

PORTER, Stanley, E., HAYES, Michael A., and TOMBS, David, eds. *Images of Christ: Ancient and Modern* (Sheffield UK: Sheffield Academic Press, 1997).

RAPLEY, Elizabeth. *The Dévotes: Women and Church in Seventeenth-Century France* (Montreal QC: McGill-Queen's University Press, 1990).

RILEY, Gregory J. *One Jesus, Many Christs: How Jesus inspired not One True Christianity, but Many: The Truth about Christian Origins* (San Francisco CA: HarperSanFrancisco, 1997).

SALISBURY, Joyce E. *Perpetua's Passion: The Death and Memory of a Young Roman Woman* (New York NY: Routledge, 1997).

SANDERS, E.P. *The Historical Figure of Jesus* (London UK: Allen Lane, Penguin Press, 1993).

SCHILLEBEECKX, Edward, O.P. *Jesus in Our Western Culture: Mysticism, Ethics and Politics* (London UK: SCM Press, 1987).

SCHÜSSLER FIORENZA, Elisabeth. *Jesus: Miriam's Child, Sophia's Prophet: Critical Issues in Feminist Christology* (New York NY: Continuum, 1994).

SIMARD, Jean. *Les arts sacrés au Québec* (Boucherville QC: Éditions de Mortagne, 1989).

SIMPSON, Patricia. *Marguerite Bourgeoys and Montreal, 1640-1665* (Montreal QC: McGill-Queen's University Press, 1997).

SLOYAN, Gerard S. *The Jesus Tradition: Images of Jesus in the West* (Mystic CT: Twenty-Third Publications, 1986).

STEERE, Douglas V. *Quaker Spirituality: Selected Writings* (New York NY: Paulist Press, 1984).

STOTT, John R.W. *The Cross of Christ* (Downer's Grove, ILL: Inter-Varsity Press, 1986).

SUGIRTHARAJAH, R.S., ed. *Asian Faces of Jesus* (Maryknoll NY: Orbis Books, 1993).

TENDULKAR, Dinanath Gopal. *Mahatma: Life of Mohandas Karamchand Gandhi* (Bombay, India: Publications Division, Ministry of Information and Broadcasting, Government of India, 1951-).

THOMPSON, William M, ed. *Bérulle and the French School: Selected Writings* (New York NY: Paulist Press, 1989).

THUNBERG, Lars. *Man and the Cosmos: The Vision of St Maximus the Confessor* (Crestwood NY: St Vladimir's Seminary Press, 1985).

VLACHOS, Hierotheos S. *Orthodox Psychotherapy (The Science of the Fathers)* (Levadia, Greece: Birth of the Theotokos Monastery, 1994).

WARD, Benedicta, S.L.G. *Harlots of the Desert: A Study of Repentance in Early Monastic Sources* (Kalamazoo MI: Cistercian Publications, 1987).

WESSELS, Anton. *Images of Jesus: How Jesus is Perceived and Portrayed in Non-European Cultures* (Grand Rapids MI: William B. Eerdmans Publishing Co., 1990).

WILBERFORCE, Robert Isaac and WILBERFORCE, Samuel. *The Life of William Wilberforce* 2nd ed. (London UK: John Murray, 1872).

WOOLMAN, John. *The Journal and Essays of John Woolman* (London UK: Macmillan and Co., 1922).

ZERNOV, Nicolas. *Eastern Christendom: A Study of the Origin and Development of the Eastern Orthodox Church* (London UK: Weidenfeld and Nicolson, 1961).